Woke Free

Campus Guide for

Students, Faculty and Alumni

Establishing a "Woke Free" Environment on Campus by Abolishing DEI Bureaucracies and Restoring Equality (*NOT Equity*) in America's Universities

By

Corey Lee Wilson

Woke Free Campus Guide

Woke Free Campus Guide for Students, Faculty and Alumni

Fratire Publishing books can be purchased in bulk with special discounts for educational purposes, organizational gifts, sales promotions, and special editions can be created to specifications. All inquiries for such can be made below.

FRATIRE PUBLISHING LLC
4533 Temescal Canyon Rd. # 308
Corona, CA 92883
www.FratirePublishing.com
FratirePublishing@att.net
(951) 638-5502

FratirePublishing
Relevant Books for **SAPIENT** Beings

Fratire Publishing is all about common sense and relevant books for sapient beings. If this sounds like you and you can never have enough common sense, wisdom and relevancy, then visit us at www.FratirePublishing.com.

Printed paperback and eBook ePUB by Ingram Spark in La Vergne, Tennessee, USA
Copyright © 2024: April 2024
ISBN 978-0-9994017-8-1 (Paperback)
ISBN 978-1-953319-41-8 (eBook)
WFCG-01-PDF (pdf)
WFCG-01-EPUB (epub)
LCCN 2024906709

Book cover logo by dasignlady at:
https://www.redbubble.com/people/dasignlady/shop?artistUserName=dasignlady&iaCode=all-stickers.

Contents

Acknowledgements

Below are the major contributors to *Woke Free Campus Guide for Students, Faculty and Alumni* that were borrowed from, verbatim, quoted, and conceptualized, from a little to a lot. Wherever this happened, their contributions and sources are acknowledged in the Resources section at the end of the book, as well as the Index section, and done intentionally so as to not distract the reader from the themes and messages covered throughout the chapters of the handbook.

Christopher F. Rufo – Is an American conservative activist, contributing editor of *City Journal,* New College of Florida board member, senior fellow at the Manhattan Institute for Policy Research, and leading the fight against Progressivism madness in American institutions. He is a vocal opponent of critical race theory, former documentary filmmaker and fellow at the Discovery Institute, the Claremont Institute, The Heritage Foundation, and the Foundation Against Intolerance and Racism. In 2022, he earned a Master of Liberal Arts in Extension Studies from Harvard Extension School.

City Journal: Is a public policy magazine and website, published by the Manhattan Institute for Policy Research, that covers a range of topics on urban affairs, such as policing, education, housing, and other issues. The *City Journal* and its authors were the most widely used resource for *Education Madness.*

Heritage Foundation, The – Is an American conservative think tank that is primarily geared toward public policy and the foundation took a leading role in the conservative movement during the presidency of Ronald Reagan, whose policies were taken from Heritage's policy study Mandate for Leadership. The Heritage Foundation has partnered with congruent organizations to provide various model legislation, including their own, that states can use to protect education freedom. Their Save Our Schools Parental Rights Resources are extensive with instructional, legislative, and school board training resources.

S.A.P.I.E.N.T. Being – The Society Advancing Personal Intelligence and Enlightenment Now Together (S.A.P.I.E.N.T.) Being is the leading anti-woke and anti-progressivism madness organization and think tank in the USA. They publish *Education Madness: A SAPIENT Being's Guide to Fixing America's Dysfunctional & Illiberal Educational Systems*, a textbook from their Sapient Conservative Textbook (SCT) Program, an alternative social studies textbooks program to counter woke and progressive madness in America's educational institutions, and help return conservative values, viewpoint diversity, and sapience to high school and college campuses.

A Woke Free Campus Introduction

Leaders of elite schools disgrace themselves before Congress—and expose the rot at the core of American higher education after being summoned to account for the surging anti-Semitism on their campuses, the presidents of Harvard, MIT, and the University of Pennsylvania delivered a masterclass in obfuscation.

As noted in the Liel Leibovitz "The Big University Fail" *City Journal* December 2023 report: When New York representative Elise Stefanik asked them whether calling for the genocide of the Jewish people violated the codes of conduct of their respective institutions, for example, all three presidents responded by saying that—well, it's complicated.

"It is a context-dependent decision," Penn's Liz Magill answered, driving Stefanik—and anyone else watching with half a heart and a brain—to wonder just what was so difficult or context-dependent about cheering for the murder of every Jewish man, woman, and child.

The hearing made headlines, and rightly so. But it would be a mistake to focus on the trio's failure to sound remotely empathic when discussing the safety and wellbeing of their Jewish students. The problem with Harvard, Penn, MIT, and others isn't merely that these previously august institutions condone, or at the very least tolerate, anti-Semitism. It goes much deeper, and you could sum it up in three letters: DEI—or diversity, equity, and inclusion, the ongoing effort to regulate a host of policies pertaining to race, sexual orientation, and other identity markers.

Consider Harvard. Our nation's most lauded university is currently home to 7,240 undergraduate students and 7,024 administrators, or nearly one administrator for each young adult. Some of these officials, it's possible, are doing important work. But if you're wondering what the rest are up to, you needn't look much further than the *Crimson*, the university's long-running student newspaper. Recently, the *Harvard Crimson* reported on the Faculty of Arts and Sciences (FAS) Task Force on Visual Culture and Signage, created on the recommendation of the Presidential Task Force on Inclusion and Belonging. The Visual Culture and Signage task force's 24 members, including nine administrators, toiled for months and interviewed more than 500 people before delivering a 26-page report that included recommendations like one urging Harvard to "clarify institutional authority over FAS visual culture and signage." This farce ended the only way it could have—with the minting of a new administrative post, the FAS campus curator, and a new committee, the FAS Standing Committee on Visual Culture and Signage, to help facilitate the curator's all-important work.

It's easy to laugh all this off as fussy ivory tower nonsense, but DEI isn't just another campus pastime. It's a mechanism for the forging and dissemination of an ideological construct that, before the progressive assault on words and their meaning, used to be called racism. Or, for that matter, anti-Semitism: singling out Jews or the Jewish state for calumny used to be frowned upon, but, under the aegis of DEI, it passes as a respectable, even essential pursuit.

That's because, as Stanley Goldfarb explained in *City Journal* recently, "at the heart of DEI is a simple binary: the world is divided between oppressors and the oppressed." And Jews confound these categories because Judaism is both a belief system and an extended family with roots everywhere from Yemen to Yekaterinburg.

None of DEI's grotesque simplifications holds up when applied to the Jews, which is why the Jews must be singled out for scorn. Take these ancient, stiff-necked people and their persistent faith seriously, and the whole con collapses. Write them off as just a particularly nefarious example of whites exercising undue power and influence on poor people of color somewhere far away, and your thwarted worldview can remain undisturbed.

Delivering what was possibly the congressional hearing's most poignant moment, Utah representative Burgess Owens asked the university presidents a series of simple questions. "Harvard now has graduations for black-only graduates, Hispanic-only graduates, and gay-only graduates," he asked Harvard's Claudine Gay. "How does that bring us together as opposed to dividing us based on color, creed, and all the other things? And, by the way, is it okay for a white group to say 'we don't want minorities to be a part of our graduation'?"

Gay started in on an evasive response, but Burgess cut her off.

"Is it okay to segregate people based on their color?" he asked.

"I oppose segregation," Gay replied.

"Okay," Owens shot back, "I do, too. But it's happening on your campus."

This Grand Guignol went on for many minutes, with every president loudly denouncing separating students based on the color of their skin yet failing to explain why such separation was appropriate on their campuses when practiced by minority groups. You hardly needed a Ph.D. from MIT to realize that the presidents' declamations were idiotic. But anyone watching might have been excused for asking just why these formerly venerable institutions would stoop so low as to peddle such rank illogic.

Sincere ideological conviction, of course, provides one answer. It's possible that Gay and her colleagues truly believe that black-only dorms are good, while similar set-ups by those with a different skin color is racism. But there's another explanation, too, and it has to do with money.

Earlier this year, three partners in the management consulting firm Bain and Company published a rousing defense of DEI in the Harvard Business Review. Their argument wasn't that DEI made organizations more just, or society more diverse, equitable, or inclusive. It was that DEI helped enhance an organization's "change power," or its ability to be more adaptable and profitable in the marketplace.

By that metric, our universities have change superpowers. In 1969, for example, about 78 percent of faculty members in American universities and colleges held tenured or tenure-track positions. Today, the number is roughly 20 percent, which means that the majority of classes are taught by poorly paid adjuncts. A decade ago, when I was still a professor at NYU, two-thirds of the classes in my department were taught by adjuncts (the university-wide rate is about 53 percent), who earned, on average, something like $800 a month. Even the most dedicated adjuncts could not afford to invest too much time and energy in their students' education.

It should come as no surprise, then, that the overall quality of a university education has plummeted. One federal survey, conducted about a decade ago, tested the literacy (defined as "using printed and written information to function in society, to achieve one's goals and to develop one's knowledge and potential") of college-educated Americans. It found that only a quarter of those surveyed met these basic criteria.

At the same time, our universities found new and exciting ways to make money. The easiest way was to hike tuition: in 2001, the cost of a university education was 23 percent of median annual earnings. By 2011, the number had reached 38 percent, and student debt, as if by design, doubled.

But students and their parents are a relatively limited and non-renewable source of revenue, which is why American universities learned the same lesson that helped make, say, Arby's or Wendy's great—if you want to grow big, sell franchises. To name just one example of many, NYU has twin degree-granting campuses in Abu Dhabi and in Shanghai, as well as locations in Accra, Berlin, Buenos Aires, Florence, London, Los Angeles, Madrid, Paris, Prague, Sydney, Tel Aviv, and Washington, D.C. No cluster of wealthy people need go far to acquire the prestige of an NYU degree.

If you think of students as consumers, as American universities now do, DEI is a convenient organizing principle, not only tapping into trends that animate the young but also replacing that stubborn and unruly thing—an independent community of scholars dedicated to one another and to the unfettered exchange of ideas—with atomized clusters of competing identity groups, all depending on the administration for validation and resources. If you want to cultivate perpetual clients eager to pay for the privilege of your validation, just give each client an administrator.

It's no wonder, then, that Penn president Magill smirked when confronted with her university's moral failings. She likely realizes, as so many others have yet to do, that American universities are no longer interested in the improvement of minds, hearts, and souls but rather in the fattening of coffers that becomes possible when you're an integral part of the global corporate complex. As for the Jews? They are, as always, the canary in the coal mine: institutions that turn on the Jews usually expedite their own spectacular implosion. If history is any guide, this week, in Washington, we witnessed the beginning of another such episode.

1 – Where Did Wokeness Come From? Who Are These Progressives?

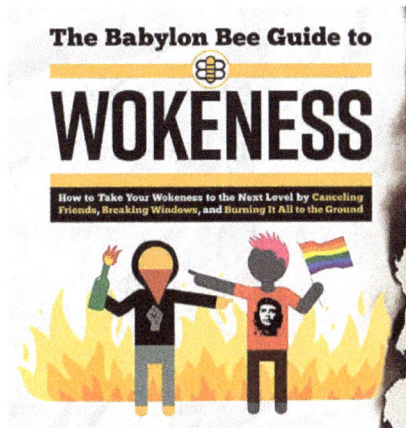

Credit: Babylon Bee.

As extensively documented, our universities have been swept up into a new cultural movement, the so-called "social justice" movement, a key component of wokeness.

"Social justice" ideology is based on the Marxist vision that the world is divided into oppressor classes and oppressed classes as noted in the Minding the Campus article "What Happened to Our Universities?" by Philip Carl Salzman, in October 2018 and is from their Free Speech in Peril collection.

Unlike classical Marxism that divides the world into a bourgeois oppressor class and a proletarian oppressed class — that is capitalists oppressing workers — neo-Marxist "social justice" theory divides the world into gender, racial, sexual, and religious classes: male oppressors and female victims; white oppressors and people of color victims; heterosexual oppressors and gay, lesbian, transsexual, etc. etc. victims; Christian and Jewish oppressors and Muslim victims.

"Social justice" ideology leads to the rejection of oppressive institutions such as capitalism and Western Civilization. Universalistic criteria such as merit, achievement, and excellence are rejected today in universities and beyond because they allegedly disadvantage members of victim categories.

What Happened to Our Universities?

Preferential measures on behalf of victims have been adopted as the overriding and primary purpose of universities today. Course topics, course substance, course references, recruitment of students, provision of special facilities and events for "victim" categories, hiring of academic and administrative staff, all are aimed to benefit members of "victim" categories and to exclude and marginalize members of "oppressor" categories.

Sociology, anthropology, political science, English, history, women's and gender studies, black studies, social work, education, and law have all jettisoned their traditional fields of study to become "social justice" subjects, vilifying men, whites, heterosexuals, the West, capitalism, and advocating for women, people of color, gays etc., and Muslims.

Now there is a full-throttle attack on the natural sciences and on STEM fields to infuse them with "victims," whatever these "victim" preferences and abilities might be, and to turn STEM into "social justice" fields, so that there would no longer be "science," but "feminist science" that is "socially just."

How did all of this happen? What brought about this almost universal change in institutions of "higher learning"?

Given the normality of closed absolutist theological and moral systems, nothing is so abnormal in human history and culture as an open, self-correcting system. Among all the cultures of the world throughout history, the only two self-correcting systems known are products of the Enlightenment: science and democracy.

Science and its technological offspring were slow to develop, but by the 20th century, they were central to Western society, while religion was removed from societal institutions and limited to the personal. This did not stop closed ideological movements such as Nazism and Communism from appropriating science and technology to advance their absolutist ideological goals. But with the self- destruction of Nazism and Communism,

8

science itself has remained an open culture.

Since the eclipse of theology in the 19th century, science has been the backbone of higher education in the West. As the most successful method for understanding the world, it was taken as a model for most academic work. Throughout the 19th and 20th centuries, social studies emulated the natural sciences, as best they could, in the hope of producing valid findings.

Academics commonly feel that they cannot simply repeat what their teachers and the founders of their field said. To gain any attention and stature, academics, especially in the social sciences and humanities, must come up with something original to say.

Furthermore, while natural scientists can express their creativity by discovering or refining a relationship between natural phenomena, social scientists and humanists do not get very far by dwelling on ethnographic or statistical or historical details. Rather, to make a splash, they must invent a new theory, a new "ism," a new epistemology. So new theoretical arguments in the social sciences and humanities tend to come not from responding to the bulk of scientific evidence, but from professional and career considerations.

By the 1980s, the social sciences and humanities had taken what some called "the postmodern turn," also characterized as a "paradigm shift." This included a rejection of attempts to be objective, and, in its place, a celebration of subjectivity.

Absoluteness, as in absolute truth, was rejected in favor of relativism. Academics came to say that "everyone has their own truth." Science was rejected as a model for studies of humanity. The ideas of "data" and "evidence" were set aside in favor of "interpretation." Scientific laws, generalizations, and "master narratives," were rejected as unfeasible and oppressive.

Anthropology's contributions to this turn were substantial. "Cultural relativism," which had been conceptualized in the first half of the 20th century by Franz Boas and Ruth Benedict as a mental attitude to make researchers more receptive to understanding cultures other than their own, had morphed into moral relativism by the second half of the 20th century as shown by the rejection of the United Nations Universal Declaration of Human Rights by the American Anthropological Association on the grounds that it was based on Western cultural ideas.

9

The most influential anthropologist of the second half of the 20th century, Clifford Geertz, who was followed closely in all the social sciences and humanities, turned away from cultural anthropology as a scientific study, instead likening it to literary criticism.

Perhaps Geertz was influenced in this by deconstructionism, fashionable in literary studies. The main thrust of Geertz's theory was that, in ethnographic research, we interpret what we see and hear, and present that interpretation as our understanding. In the much-lauded Introduction of *The Interpretation of Cultures*, Geertz says that "what we call our data are really our own constructions of other people's constructions of what they and their compatriots are up to." This is reflected in his famous definition of culture:

"The concept of culture I espouse,…is essentially a semiotic one. Believing, with Max Weber, that man is an animal suspended in webs of significance he himself has spun, I take culture to be those webs, and the analysis of it to be therefore not an experimental science in search of law but an interpretative one in search of meaning."

With the scientific spirit rejected by the social sciences and humanities, and the idea of authoritative knowledge rejected in favor of allegedly valid subjective truths, what role can the university play? The discovery and passing on of new knowledge have, in the postmodern turn, been judged invalid.

In the absence of knowledge, what then is the purpose of research and scholarship and teaching? The answer was found in turn to moralism and political activism. This drew on the critical Marxist anthropology of the 1970s and came to fruition in the most popular anthropology book of the 1980s, *Anthropology as Cultural Critique* by George E. Marcus and Michael M. J. Fischer.

In the following decades, the neo-Marxist "social justice" ideology and movement flowered. Our society is condemned in universities for being racist, sexist, homophobic, Islamophobic, and oppressive.

To correct this, professors and administrators advocate for programs benefitting the "victims of oppression," that is, females, people of color, gays—lesbian—transsexuals, etc., and Muslims, such as preferential admission for student applicants, separate housing, eating, and support facilities, special ceremonies, and preferential hiring as professors and administrators.

The disfavored "oppressors," males, whites, heterosexuals, and Christians are to be marginalized and sidelined, certainly not to receive any benefits or opportunities. (Asians are now honorary whites because they have worked too hard and are too successful, so they too are condemned and discriminated against.)

The rejection of truth and of evidence has now made its way into university administrations. Disciplinary tribunals have now accepted that "everyone has their own truth," and they accept the "truths" of the oppressed victims and dispense with "evidence" that might be presented on behalf of accused "oppressors."

This rejection of truth and evidence has diffused far beyond universities, to businesses, funding agencies, government agencies, and departments of education, and has now made its way to the U.S. Senate in the Kavanaugh hearings. What someone did or did not do is no longer important; the only thing that is important in universities and beyond is what category someone belongs to. After all, that is the only way that "social justice" is enforced.

Universities Must Choose One Telos: Truth or Social Justice

On the Heterodox Academy website, Dr. Jonathan Haidt explains eloquently why universities must choose one telos: truth or social justice. Furthermore, he elaborates that Aristotle often evaluated a thing with respect to its "telos"–its purpose, end, or goal. The telos of a knife is to cut. The telos of a physician is health or healing. What is the telos of university?

The most obvious answer is "truth"—the word appears on so many university crests. But increasingly, many of America's top universities are embracing social justice as their telos, or as a second and equal telos. But can any institution or profession have two teloses (or teloi)? What happens if they conflict?

Haidt believes that the conflict between truth and social justice is likely to become unmanageable. Universities will have to choose, and be explicit about their choice, so that potential students and faculty recruits can make an informed choice. Universities that try to honor both will face increasing incoherence and internal conflict.

To further illuminate his point, consider two quotations:

The philosophers have only interpreted the world, in various ways; the point is to change it.– Karl Marx, 1845

He who knows only his own side of the case knows little of that. His reasons may be good, and no one may have been able to refute them. But if he is equally unable to refute the reasons on the opposite side, if he does not so much as know what they are, he has no ground for preferring either opinion…– John Stuart Mill, 1859

As Haidt puts it: Marx is the patron saint of what he calls "Social Justice U," which is oriented around changing the world in part by overthrowing power structures and privilege. It sees political diversity as an obstacle to action.

Mill is the patron saint of what he calls "Truth U," which sees truth as a process in which flawed individuals challenge each other's biased and incomplete reasoning. In this process, all become smarter. However, Truth U dies when it becomes intellectually uniform or politically orthodox.

What's it Going to Be: Truth or Social Justice?

Truth is paramount to sapience, and the antithesis to sapience is modern progressivism. Not only does progressivism deny commonly held truths across all cultures of the world, today's progressivism has evolved to many degrees into a twentieth century version of Marxism lite—without the horrific calories of human sacrifice, failed regimes, and economic ruin.

When progressivism madness is incubated in the right condition on campus, illiberalism will follow, and when illiberalism follows, so do social justice warriors and campus radicals. Put simply enough by Haidt, "no university can have Truth and Social Justice as dual teloses. Each university must pick one.

Universities Have Become Ground Zero for the Progressive Neo-Racism of DEI

Critical race theorists have been dominant in colleges and universities for years, but their impact on public policy was limited until recently. The precepts of CRT have now burst outside the universities, affecting K-12 schools, workplaces, state and federal governments, and even the military. This has sparked resistance from Americans who refuse to have their children indoctrinated or to submit to race-based workplace harassment.

As a new tactic against this grassroots opposition, CRT's defenders now deny that the curricula and training programs in question form part of CRT, insisting that the "diversity, equity, and inclusion (DEI)" programs of trainers such as Ibram X. Kendi and Robin DiAngelo are distinct from the academic work of professors such as Derrick Bell, Kimberle Crenshaw, and other CRT architects.

While there are many different CRT variations, there are bedrock features that are common to all its theorists and practitioners such as the cult of race and gender victimology, and this diversity cult is systematically destroying the social fabric of our multi-racial society, the equality of opportunity that makes that possible, and America's unifying cultural cohesion. It is worth first exploring, however, why social-justice education is an oxymoron.

This new academic state religion of DEI combines the ideology of intersectionality with strands of radical feminism, anti-imperialism, and gay and transgender activism as noted in the Howard Gold "Opinion: At America's most 'woke' colleges, extreme liberal politics fails students and free speech" Market Watch article published in January 2020:

But it's really about turning the existing power relationships on their head, so that, say, black lesbians or trans women are now at the top of the inverted pyramid and "cis" white males are at the bottom. "Toxic masculinity" and "white privilege" are the roots of all evil. The last shall be first, and the first last.

It's true that men have dominated the world and women lag behind; gay people have been persecuted, trans people continue to be targets of violence, and African-Americans and other people of color are still victims of systemic racism and discrimination in jobs, housing, and policing. But self-righteous undergraduates, backed by professors and administrators, are turning this new campus orthodoxy into a toxic stew. "Four legs good, two legs bad," the sheep brayed in *Animal Farm*. Once again, life imitates Orwell.

Where Did Wokeness Come From?

Per the Theodore Kupfer "Where Did Wokeness Come From?" *City Journal* August 2022 article:

Wokeness, most observers would agree, can be defined as the progressive worldview that views all racial and sexual disparities as proof of discrimination, and rejects liberal procedural traditions in favor of a totalizing politics that seeks to dismantle those disparities and silence dissenters.

But nobody seems to agree on where it came from.

Is wokeness an intellectual, religious, psychological, economic, legal, or institutional phenomenon? Its emergence over the last decade or so has been attributed to everything from academic intellectual trends, declining religiosity, victimhood psychology, corporate self-interest, white-collar class interests, the civil rights laws of the 1960s, and the copycat tendencies of large organizations. These all seem to have some explanatory power, but none seems on its own to account for the phenomenon fully. Let's consider each in turn.

Ideas have consequences

The idealist account sees wokeness as the offspring of long-gestating intellectual trends. The specifics might vary, but the broad story tends to be the same: influential thinkers developed a critique of reason, objectivity, and neutrality that conquered the ivory tower before infecting everyone from Democratic Party politicians to the editors of *Teen Vogue*.

Whether it was Immanuel Kant, Theodor Adorno, or Jacques Derrida, some philosopher started the process by arguing that humans had insufficient grounds to believe things they once took for granted, since those beliefs were filtered—and distorted—by limited individual faculties, cultural biases, or "systems of power and hierarchies, which decide what can be known and how."

That critical posture toward established truths challenged the foundations of Enlightenment civilization and encouraged a vision of the world as divided among "oppressed classes" and an "oppressor class."

In an American context, the critique took various forms, with radical feminists arguing that the legal system was "a medium for making male dominance both invisible and legitimate" and critical race theorists maintaining that racism represents "the usual way [American] society does business, the common, everyday experience of most people of color in this country."

14

These kinds of arguments eventually entered public debate as default explanations for inequalities in American society; American institutions came to be seen solely as vectors of subjugation.

Idealist accounts leave something important unexplained, however: How did these ideas spread?

In a review of James Lindsay and Helen Pluckrose's *Cynical Theories*, a representative idealist account, critic Park MacDougald notes that the book never explains how people came to be persuaded by fundamentally unpersuasive arguments.

"At times, Pluckrose and Lindsay write as if these theories are free-floating ideas developing according to their own internal logic. At times, they are analogized to a virus jumping the 'species gap' from academia to activism. And at times, there's no clear agent at all, as when they write that Evergreen State 'got overtaken by the ideas of critical race theory,'" MacDougald writes.

"But how does a college get overtaken by ideas? And why one set of ideas instead of another?"

The idealist account, on its own, seems unable to answer these questions.

Psychological accounts

Two explanations argue that wokeness has gained traction in response to specific changes in Americans' psychology.

One posits that wokeness resembles a religion, filling a spiritual vacuum in American life. Author John McWhorter argues that "third-wave antiracism . . . has actually become a religion," complete with a clergy in the form of writers such as Ibram X. Kendi and Ta-Nehisi Coates, a creed holding that "racism is baked into the structure of society," and a creation myth involving the African slave trade.

Another sees it as a byproduct of the infantilization of young Americans by well-meaning but overprotective parents. In the best-selling *The Coddling of the American Mind*, Greg Lukianoff and Jonathan Haidt blame "safetyism"—which puts a premium on protection of feelings and punishes severely actions or words that inflict emotional harm—as a proximate cause of political strife on college campuses.

Lukianoff and Haidt weren't offering a catch-all theory of wokeness, but their story—that an overprotective mode of parenting that took hold in the late twentieth century produced a generation of hypersensitive kids, who then entered a bureaucratized college system willing to meet their demands for "safe spaces"—is a reasonable stand-in for those who view wokeness as a form of political activism common to millennials and zoomers.

Still, neither theory seems dispositive

First, pathologizing particular ideas or beliefs as the product of a specific psychological makeup is a reductive and unfalsifiable move (as with the notion, dating back to Adorno in the 1950s, that the political views of American conservatives are merely symptoms of an "authoritarian" personality type).

Neither the *religious* nor the *victimhood* argument quite succeeds on its own terms: wokeness tends to go awry not by making unverifiable supernatural claims but by making false empirical ones; and psychological changes seem insufficient to explain why woke students came to adopt an identity-based obsession with statistical disparities as opposed to, say, a militant socialist politics. And woke beliefs aren't held only by true believers or college students.

Incentives

Into this breach step two materialist explanations, alleging that woke politics in the corporate environment serves the incentives of economic actors.

First is the "woke capital" thesis, which maintains that executives adopt a woke posture—moving operations out of red states, endorsing the outlandish rhetoric of diversity trainers—to make money.

- Maybe a company's endorsement of the idea that the United States is founded on the plunder of black bodies enables it to attract more talent, as it's hiring from a small pool of young people with top-notch educational credentials, whose worldview tends to be similarly woke.

- Maybe a company's declaration of a solemn commitment to social responsibility allows it to exploit a growth field, as in the creation of ESG funds by financial firms.

- Or maybe executives are preempting a potential anti-capitalist upsurge from the political Left.

Ross Douthat argued in the *New York Times* that "corporate activism on social issues" serves to "justify the ways of C.E.O.s to cultural power brokers, so that those same power brokers will leave them alone . . . in realms that matter more to the corporate bottom line."

Former biotech CEO Vivek Ramaswamy develops the argument in *Woke, Inc.*, offering a potted history in which corporations nervous about growing redistributionist sentiment on the left following the 2008 financial crisis struck a bargain with identity-obsessed activists, taking up their cherished claims in exchange for being left alone.

This, too, seems insufficient

As Josh Barro notes, corporate employees aren't motivated by profit alone: they might introduce politics to the workplace because of their own political views. Indeed, many high-profile instances of corporations groveling to activists and stifling internal dissent from the company line were driven from below, not above.

The ouster of Mozilla CEO Brendan Eich for his opposition to gay marriage, Google firing James Damore for his memo on innate gender differences, the *New York Times* buckling to a staff revolt over a Republican politician's op-ed, *Bon Appetit* disbanding its video department over staff allegations of unequal pay, and the CEO of Disney attacking a Florida law on sex education in elementary schools only after a staff revolt: in all these cases, the pressure seemed to come from within the organization.

Another materialist account, the "woke labor" thesis, promises to explain such cases. In short, a glut of well-educated but insecure white-collar workers use their control over corporate resources to push a political agenda that they not only agree with but also depend upon for job security.

In *City Journal*, Malcom Kyeyune writes that America's culture wars can be understood by examining the class interests of mid-level managers who don't own capital but retain control over how it is deployed. What seem like earnest arguments for a company allegedly dogged by a toxic culture to submit to an audit or scale up its diversity-training initiatives actually constitute calls for a "massive expansion of managerial intermediation in previously independent social and economic processes."

These managers simply want to create more work for themselves (and other members of their guild). Cancellations of dissenters therefore function as labor market discipline, forcing the unwoke to exit the sector.

But how can economic incentives explain the great many cancellations that have little to do with material gain, as in hobbyist communities like knitting? These cases suggest an ideological dimension to wokeness that the materialist explanations cannot capture.

Explicit instances of coordination between corporations and activists also tend to be lacking. And, after all, woke boilerplate tends to identify capitalism as one of many interlocking systems of oppression that keep minorities down.

Institutional accounts

The legalist account ties wokeness to various American civil rights laws whose vagueness, and selective enforcement, cowed organizations into compliance with an ever-expanding array of prohibitions on free speech and political disagreement in order to avoid the prospect of litigation.

The Civil Rights Act of 1964 marks the beginning of this history. Its bans on discrimination according to race and gender were soon expanded by the Supreme Court to include anything that had a disparate impact on protected groups. Meantime, affirmative-action programs expanded across government and higher education, on the assumption that disparities among groups wouldn't exist absent discrimination—a central claim today.

What we think of as "political correctness" is really "a name for the cultural effect of the basic enforcement powers of civil rights law," argues Christopher Caldwell, which enabled "government censorship . . . through a civil court system that had seen its scope and punitive capacities enhanced by civil rights law" and threatened litigation that terrified employers into "privatizing the suppression of disagreement."

In *Inventing Equal Opportunity*, Harvard sociologist Frank Dobbin writes that the "continuing ambiguity of compliance standards led management writers to advocate permanent antidiscrimination offices to track legal shifts." This legal enforcement mechanism explains a great deal of corporate behavior, as political scientist Richard Hanania observes: from human-resources departments that police uncouth opinions at the office to corporations suddenly declaring their support for trendy causes when the prospect of government intervention is raised.

A rigorous thesis with much explanatory power, the legalist account nevertheless seems to leave a few things unexplained.

First, one might expect people and organizations hounded by an intrusive government apparatus to get with the program only begrudgingly, doing the bare minimum to remain in compliance. But woke organizations zealously go above and beyond what's compulsory, saying and doing things that even the vague and expanding civil rights regime doesn't require.

Second, the legal structures alleged to be the culprit for organizational wokeness have been around for decades—yet the intensity of the culture war has ramped up considerably only in the last few years.

To the rescue comes a sociological modification of the legalist account

The concept of institutional isomorphism explains the maddening tendency of organizations to update their operations for the newest woke dictates, whether it's a sudden expansion of the LGBTQ+ acronym or the need to release increasingly shrill statements about racism being endemic to American life.

The sociologist Gabriel Rossman describes in *City Journal* how "organizations go beyond their core competencies to imitate market leaders and to meet the demands of their trading partners, the regulatory state, and key employees." Institutions go woke not just because they're coerced to do so but also because peer institutions are doing it.

Meantime, as Charles Fain Lehman explains, late-twentieth-century efforts to remain in compliance with civil rights laws soon gave way to a "business case" that diversity would itself bring benefits to the corporate bottom line. "The transition from compliance to diversity marks the moment at which race-conscious corporate policy became unmoored from rational purpose and mutated into a myth," Lehman writes, noting that the evidence underlying the business case was never strong. And once such race-conscious policies became a myth, they were free to accumulate new tenets as myths do.

Each explanation for wokeness's rise has gaps that invite corrections or modifications

Left with a set of theories that don't seem to work on their own but complement each other well, one could embrace a synthesis: a perfect-storm view, in which all these different phenomena happen at once.

Thus, a certain brand of overprotective parent raised a generation of kids susceptible, in an era of declining religiosity, to morally urgent ideologies. The theory-suffused academy was happy to supply such an ideology, which these kids took up with gusto upon arriving on campus, despite its evident shortcomings.

When they graduated and started entering the white-collar work force, litigation-averse corporations—already seasoned in adjusting their behavior to comply with civil rights laws—happily indulged the political demands of this socially engaged class of workers. And, thanks to the immense cultural power of well-educated Americans and the economic power of large companies, that ideology became increasingly visible, and eventually all but inescapable.

This multifactor explanation may strike some as overthought and extravagant, but a complex account, involving many different proximate causes, somehow fits such a nebulous, yet expansive, phenomenon as wokeness. Skeptics of wokeness tend to point to the difficulty of defining it and explaining its causes, but such imprecision would be expected if it was really a number of different but interrelated and overlapping phenomena, each with its own set of causes.

What is wokeness, or being woke? The *Oxford English Dictionary* describes it as an alertness "to racial or social discrimination and injustice," and it's a term progressives and liberals aspire to be—while conservatives view it as akin to a joke, and sometimes, a social evil, like cancel culture. A sapient definition could be: "At its heart, wokeness is divisive, exclusionary, and hateful. It basically gives mean people a shield to be mean and cruel, armored in false virtue," as stated by X/Twitter CEO, Elon Musk.

2 – The Leftist Madness of Progressively Woke
Illiberal Campuses

shutterstock.com · 1036576444

In the 21st century, Progressives have innovated in ideology, jettisoning the economic class struggle of Marxism and replacing it with identity classes: gender, race, sexuality, religion, nationality, and ableness. Now it's (allegedly) whites (including "white adjacent" Asians and "hyperwhite" Jews), males, and Christians who are oppressors—and people of color, women, LGBTQ++, Muslims, and the disabled who are the oppressed victims.

With the "social justice" trinity of "diversity, equity, and inclusion," Progressives have returned us to the days of deep Jim Crow, with some races seen as virtuous and others as evil, the only difference being that the colors have changed. Progressive "inclusion" means including preferred races and genders, and excluding the others, as we see in hiring, college admissions, funding, promotions, and awards.

Equity, meaning the statistical equivalence of races and genders, in practice means more of the preferred and fewer of the despised. Objective measures, such as standardized tests, and advanced education programs, are cancelled, because they don't produce the desired "equity" results.

Now institutionalized DEI racism and discrimination are regarded as desirable by Progressives, as long as preferred categories benefit.

Who are these Progressives? Answer: They are typically very liberal, highly educated, and majority White—and most say U.S. institutions need to be completely rebuilt because of racial bias. What devious force brought all of this cultural destruction into being? Who injected this destructive poison into the Progressivism movement? The source, of course, is our universities where so many academics and college faculty are the post-modernists, pushing "Progressive" activism at a college near you.

Enough! Now is the time to wake up before we do even graver damage—not only to ourselves individually but to our country as a whole. It's a bitter irony that those who want to drive us into this new hysteria often claim to be "woke." But there is no awakening in woke. It's the sleep of reason that produces monsters, and it poses a profound peril to our republic.

National Suicide by Education–Care of Progressives

From the "National Suicide by Education–Care of Progressives" The S.A.P.I.E.N.T. Being Newsletter September 2023 article:

You may not realize it, but you might be currently funding some dangerous people. Academia is indoctrinating young minds throughout the West with their resentment-ridden ideology. They have made it their life's mission to undermine Western civilization itself, which they regard as corrupt, oppressive and "patriarchal."

If you're a taxpayer—or paying for your kid's liberal arts degree—you're underwriting this gang of nihilists. Nihilism is a philosophy, or family of views within philosophy, that rejects generally accepted or fundamental aspects of human existence, such as objective truth, knowledge, morality, values, or meaning. Supporting ideologues who claim that all truth is subjective; that all sex differences are socially constructed; and that Western imperialism is the sole source of all Third World problems—is problematic.

Many academics and college faculty are the post-modernists, pushing "progressive" activism at a college near you. They produce the mobs that violently shut down campus speakers; the language police who enshrine into law use of fabricated gender pronouns; and the deans whose livelihoods depend on madly rooting out discrimination where little or none exists.

Their thinking took hold in Western universities in the '60s and '70s when the true believers of the radical left became the professors of today. And now we rack up education-related debt—not so that our children learn to think critically, write clearly, or speak properly, but so they can model their mentors' destructive agenda.

Academia is Indoctrinating Young Minds With Their Resentment-Ridden Ideology

We now teach our children that our country is illegitimate, based on genocide and racism, and is systemically evil. Will this lead the next generation to love or despise their country? Who will volunteer for the military, to risk their lives to protect their evil country? When generals assert that the military is racist and sexist, homophobic and transphobic, and harbors white supremacists and domestic terrorists, who will volunteer for the military, to risk their lives to protect their country? Recruitment for the military in both the United States and Canada is severely down, and no one can figure out how to increase it.

We teach our children that our society is divided between helpless victims and cruel oppressors. BIPOC (black, indigenous, people of color) and females are all and everywhere oppressed, and whites and males, Christians and Jews, and (astonishingly) Asians are privileged, evil villains. Children learn to fear and hate their fellow citizens of other races, sexes, religions, and ethnicities. What kind of society will we have when we teach children that race hatred, sexism, and ethno-supremacy are justified and virtuous?

What devious force brought all of this cultural destruction into being? Who injected this destructive poison into our educational system? The source, of course, is our universities. They were taken over by grievance studies advanced by various particular interest groups. First and most decisive were the feminists who established women's and gender studies to advance what they defined as the narrow interests of women.

They adopted the Marxist model of society divided into two warring classes; in place of the proletariat versus the bourgeoisie, they defined the conflicting classes as females versus the patriarchy, all men. The feminists inspired queer studies and LGBTQ+ activism. Black studies, Latinx studies,

23

and Asian studies all championed their races in alleged conflict with the other races. Universities no longer were about what can we learn about the world and its people, but about what you could do through propaganda and activism to advance the narrow interests of your category.

All of these activisms were absorbed in social science and humanities programs, often by joint appointed professors with one or another grievance study. Administrators were either activists themselves or were won over and instituted "social justice" measures of "diversity, equity, and inclusion," hiring "diversity officers" to police the staff and students to ensure that no "wrong think" was allowed to flourish.

Faculties of education, being weak in academic content and lax in pursuing that, adopted grievance theory with a vengeance, and trained their students, the future school administrators and teachers, in the most radical forms of grievance activism. The faculties of education have contaminated our K-12 schools and made them what they are now.

It's true that children are our future, for good or ill, depending on their education. Ill-educate children, as we are doing in the United States and Canada, and the result will be cultural decay, social breakdown, and political decline.

Hate and Fear Are Now Major Motivators on Campus

Almost every university in North America has committed to what is called "social justice," which is the implementation of identity politics through the mechanisms of "diversity, equity, and inclusion." Identity politics divides everyone into one of two categories: evil oppressor or innocent victim.

Through official mandatory policies, universities have transformed academic culture from a quest to discover truth about the world and its beings, to the indoctrination of identity politics and enforcement of "social justice" policies.

In practice, this means the adoption of identity ideology to the exclusion and suppression of other views. An elaborate bureaucracy of "diversity and inclusion" officers are charged with policing thought, speech, and action. Activists, and those who support them, encourage active hate against their alleged oppressors: males, whites, Christians and Jews, heterosexuals, and cis-normal individuals.

How do we know this? Three ways: First, the vehement rejection of any criticism of or counter-argument to their neo-sexist/racist/bigoted ideological positions, and complete unwillingness to entertain any alternative position to their narratives. Second, the immediate use of the most hateful rhetoric imaginable to designate anyone challenging their position. Third, their immediate and unrestrained demands that the challenger be severely punished and preferably destroyed. Let us take these in order.

In response to any opinion contrary to their own, these activists do not offer counterarguments and contrary evidence. They do not claim that the facts are wrong or the position is untrue. No, they reject the opinion on identity grounds, saying that the challenge denies their existence as people, and that it makes them feel unsafe. Or just that it denies the truth of their sacred narrative, and that the complainant is therefore a heretic, any of whose words must be rejected.

The response on campus to this identity-fueled mob hate and its manifestation in attacks, condemnations, and cancellations is fear. Students fear bad grades if they do not repeat identity politics talking points, and they fear social isolation if they are attacked as enemies of "social justice." Professors fear both students and administrators, especially the "diversity and inclusion" officials whose job it is to weed out dissenters for re-education, punishment, and exile.

Self-censorship by college students is well documented in multiple surveys. A survey by the Foundation for Individual Rights and Expression (FIRE) reported that 83 percent engaged in self-censorship.

How far our colleges and universities have come! From open fellowships of research inquiry and intellectual exchange, they have become seminaries of true believers and doctrine enforcers. Identity politics has divided students, professors, and administrators into warring sexes, races, sexualities, genders, ethnicities, and ablenesses, and mandated hate between them. Admission and success, once based on academic achievement, merit, and potential, is now based on one's sex, race, sexuality, etc., and one's devotion to the identity politics "social justice" narrative. We have regressed from Enlightenment openness back to a Medieval religious order.

Statistical Disparities Among Groups Are Not Proof of Discrimination

Statistical disparities among groups are the norm in every facet of human life, including those in which discrimination cannot possibly play a role. To cling to a narrative that asserts racial discrimination as the only cause of statistical disparities turns a blind eye to reality and leads to harmful Progressivism policies.

From the Bradley Thomas "Statistical Disparities Among Groups Are Not Proof of Discrimination" Foundation for Economic Education (FEE) May 2019 report: In spite of this, however, perhaps the most prevalent pretext leftists have used for massive state coercion over the last 50 years is that disparities in outcomes between races, genders, or nationalities are de facto evidence of discrimination.

"Institutional" racism and sexism are the only possible causes of such disparities, the experts tell us. Society's prejudices and bigotry are so ingrained that only by growing the leviathan state can these negative results be corrected, they insist.

Does Disparity Entail Discrimination?

But if such disparities do arise absent discrimination perpetrated by "society," then assumptions about statistical disparities "lose their validity as evidence," Thomas Sowell notes in his book *Civil Rights: Rhetoric or Reality:*

There are many decisions wholly within the discretion of those concerned, where discrimination by others is not a factor—the choice of television programs to watch, opinions to express to poll takers, or the age at which to marry, for example. All these show pronounced patterns that differ from group to group.

The bottom line, Sowell concludes, is that "Statistical disparities extend into every aspect of human life" and that "statistical disparities are commonplace among human beings."

Income Inequality

Problems abound with how academics diagnose even seemingly straightforward measures like income inequality and discrimination.

The real issue is not with income inequality itself but with the processes put in motion in hopes of eliminating inequality.

For example, Sowell contends most income statistics are crude aggregates. The implicit assumption that the mere existence of income disparities is evidence of racial discrimination is unsubstantiated. Simply examining the average age differences among different demographics can explain away a portion of the income inequality that intellectuals proclaim exists due to discrimination. Those races and nationalities with older average ages would naturally boast higher average incomes due to being more experienced.

Adding factors like education level and personal career choices explains much of the rest.

The real issue, Sowell concludes, is not with income inequality itself but with the processes put in motion in hopes of eliminating inequality, which involve damaging government intervention and welfare programs.

Color vs. Culture

Moreover, when evaluating the "disparities are proof of discrimination" narrative, we can compare the levels of economic success among people of color. After all, a racist society just sees people of color and does not differentiate based upon different backgrounds.

As Sowell wrote, "Blacks may 'all look alike' to racists, but there are profound internal cultural differences among blacks."

As a result, comparing results for people of the same color but different culture is a valuable tool to provide an indication of other factors besides discrimination at work.

One source of data is a recent American Community Survey Report from the US Census Bureau that analyzes characteristics of selected Sub-Saharan African and Caribbean ancestry groups. Among these "ancestry groups," 60 percent or more are foreign-born.

Culture unquestionably plays a role in income and poverty disparities.

For instance, in 2012 the US poverty rate for Jamaicans was reported as 14.8 percent, Ethiopians 19.7 percent, and Nigerians 12.8 percent. All the rates were significantly lower than the rate of 28 percent for blacks as a whole.

Furthermore, the median income for Jamaican males was $41,969 and $39,155 for females; $34,018 for male Ethiopians and $30,253 for females; and $50,922 for male Nigerians and $44,874 for females.

Two of the three of these male ancestry groups noticeably out-earned the median rate of $37,526 for black males overall, while the same two groups outpaced the overall female black median income of $33,251.

Additionally, these three ancestry groups had significantly lower rates of poverty and higher median incomes than the Hispanic population.

How were these people of color, often without the benefit of growing up in America, able to clear the "barriers" of a discriminatory "system" far better than other people of color? Culture unquestionably plays a role in income and poverty disparities, even in situations comparing people of color where "discrimination" can be ruled out.

The Disparities Narrative Is a Pretext for Greater State Control

Nobody is arguing that racial or ethnic discrimination has been eliminated. But to cling to a narrative that asserts racial discrimination as the only cause of statistical disparities in measures such as income and poverty turns a blind eye to reality and leads to harmful policies.

Perhaps making matters worse is the promotion of the narrative of an all-powerful "system" that is structured unfairly and creates a sense of helplessness among those labeled "victims" of said barriers to economic prosperity.

"Why study and discipline yourself in preparation for the adult world if the deck is completely stacked against you anyway?" Sowell asked rhetorically.

Progressives like to lecture us about embracing diversity but then also deny that such diversity lends itself naturally to differences in outcomes. Instead, they choose to play identity politics based on faulty assumptions in pursuit of greater social control.

How American Universities Moved From Diversity to Indoctrination

This Minding the Campus article below "How a University Moved From Diversity to Indoctrination" by Daphne Patai in December 2016, is from their Free Speech in Peril collection.

Academe these days is full of code words. Diversity is one of the most popular and has increasingly become an article of faith at American colleges. Its usefulness depends on ambiguity. While the public and media may believe it means openness to previously excluded students and studies, the reality is that "diversity" is a brazen attempt at thought control, rapidly moving toward the center of undergraduate education through the mechanism of General Education requirements.

As an example, at the University of Massachusetts Amherst, professors who want their courses approved for General Education diversity credit must meet new guidelines borrowed from the most ideological part of the university, the School of Education. At UMass, as at many other universities, Social Justice Education (SJE) has for years been a key part of the School of Ed, offering not only a concentration but also a Master's and a Ph.D.

The language of SJE makes clear that it is driven by narrow political aims, which pervade all aspects of the program. With a constant emphasis on intervention and advocacy in schools and communities on behalf of social justice (never clearly defined), the SJE website makes plain its fundamental concerns, which include: "Prejudice and discrimination, the dynamics of power and privilege, and intersecting systems of oppression," "Theories and practices of social change; resistance and empowerment; liberation and social justice movements," and "Sociocultural and historical contexts for, and dynamics within and among the specific manifestations of oppression (adultism, religious oppression, ableism, classism, ethnocentrism, heterosexism, racism, sexism, transgender oppression) in educational and other social systems."

In his book *Diversity: The Invention of a Concept* (2003), Peter Wood describes how "diversity arose as a countercultural critique of American society that depicted social relations as based on hierarchy and oppression of disprivileged groups." This "diversity ideology," rooted in a Marxist view of America as a system of oppression, had been brewing for generations but only gained real traction in the 1980s.

"For it was then," he writes, "that the Left, at last, found a combination of political leverage, economic opportunity and cultural advantage to institutionalize much of its anti-American program. Diversity was the key to that three-part success" (his emphasis)."

But until recently, the emphasis on diversity as the chosen path to "social justice" was not built into the university's "social and cultural diversity" Gen Ed requirement. Now it is. And as I argue here, it is an exercise in compelled speech, unworthy of higher education, and unconstitutional in a public institution.

A fairly loose definition of what diversity courses should entail had existed for about three decades. Designed to combat "ethnocentric stereotypes" and open students to the wider world of "pluralistic perspectives," the old diversity requirements contained a single prescriptive phrase (my emphasis):

Courses satisfying this requirement shall reach beyond the perspectives of mainstream American culture and the Western tradition.

The Old Guidelines Then Shifted From Shall to May

They may focus on the peoples of Africa, Asia, Latin America, or the Middle East; the descendants of those peoples living in North America; other minorities in Western industrial societies; and Native Americans. Since sensitivity to social and cultural diversity is advanced by an understanding of the dynamics of power in modern societies, courses that focus on the differential life experiences of women outside the mainstream of American culture, minorities outside the mainstream of American culture, and the poor also come within the scope of this requirement.

True, the phrase regarding "the dynamics of power," hinting at the old Marxist framework with a touch of Foucault thrown in, seemed designed to predetermine the content of such courses to some extent. But the list of groups (women, minorities, and the poor) with "differential life experiences" was merely, as the last part of the above paragraph made clear, a possible focus–not a necessary one, and certainly nothing like the obligatory listing of numerous supposedly marginalized identities that abound today.

What, then, changed? In the spring of 2016, faculty began to realize that the General Education Council had proposed a little-publicized new delineation of the required diversity courses. As before, undergraduates would be required to take two courses carrying the Diversity designation, one national, the other international, but the details had passed through an ideological transformation.

Normally, significant changes to the curriculum would have to go through the Faculty Senate, but the Gen Ed Council had by-passed this step by claiming (when challenged) that the changes in the two required diversity courses involved "only language," hence did not need Faculty Senate approval.

Most faculty, as usual, were busy with other things and did not react. Some people, however, were alarmed. Harvey Silverglate, civil liberties attorney and co-founder of FIRE (the Foundation for Individual Rights and Expression) and I wrote a piece about the new requirement, pointing out the ways in which it went well beyond the existing guidelines. We argued that not content with existing policies that restricted speech, the university was mounting an effort to compel certain kinds of speech and political attitudes in courses hoping to gain Gen Ed Council approval toward fulfilling the diversity requirement. As we wrote:

Using politically fashionable jargon, the three new gen-ed guidelines for diversity courses stipulate not merely, as before, geographic and cultural breadth but the specific attitudes and beliefs that must animate certain areas of teaching (or indoctrination, depending upon your point of view). Faculty members must embrace "knowledge, pluralistic perspectives, and engagement beyond mainstream traditions," by focusing on "unequal access to resources that derive from race and ethnicity, national origins, language, socioeconomic class, gender and sexual orientation, religion, age, and ability."

The second mandated guideline encompasses "cultural, social and structural dynamics" that shape human experience and produce inequality, while the third specifies "exploration of self and others" so as to recognize inequalities and injustices. The clearly stated goal, not left to the imagination, is "to engage with others to create change toward social justice."

This phrase encapsulates the shift from educating students to be able to think and analyze for themselves to the vastly different effort to indoctrinate students into administrators' and professors' belief system, which is assumed to be the only worthwhile, good and moral one from which, therefore, no one dares dissent.

All of This Should Cause Concern at Public Universities That Are Bound by Constitutional Norms

The First Amendment's protection of free speech has two aspects. The more widely known one prohibits the law from censoring officially disfavored and unpopular speech. But the other equally important and complementary aspect of this liberty enjoins the government from compelling speech and belief.

In a society where students have long been granted the right to refuse, for example, to recite a biblical passage or even the Pledge of Allegiance in public schools, college students are now required to genuflect before the banner of diversity, inclusion and social justice. It's insufficient for students to refrain from uttering offensive or "wrong" words and ideas. They must increasingly be trained to mimic their professors and affirmatively utter the "right" ones.

The new guidelines, in other words, explicitly spelled out a commitment to social justice, understood in a particular way, reflecting precisely the political vision already familiar to us from Social Justice Education programs, rooted in Left politics that have dominated academic circles for some time now.

But whereas these politics used to be confined to certain (mostly identity-based) academic programs, along with Schools of Ed and Social Work, the new requirements aim to subject the entire university and every student in it to current academic dogma. The revision names identity groups repeatedly, uses all the current code words, talks over and over again about inequality, marginalization, power dynamics, and the need to combat all these.

Hardly a minor revision, this is a complete delineation of the changes in academe in the past few decades. At a time when the university persistently reiterates its commitment to social justice, diversity, inclusion, and equity, the undergraduate curriculum is undergoing Gleichschaltung, i.e., everything is being brought into alignment with the prevailing political orthodoxy.

A further chapter in this story of ideological policing unfolded in late 2016. Not satisfied with the changes quietly incorporated into the Gen Ed diversity requirement earlier in 2016, the Gen Ed Council once again initiated a change that it evidently hoped most faculty would not notice.

This time, it proposed a third required diversity course, mandated for all incoming students, who apparently needed this training in identity politics in order to proceed with their education.

I conclude that we hardly know what "social justice" is, let alone how it may best be attained. Indeed, the very term has been used in ways that might alarm today's social justice warriors (if only they knew some history, such as that of the populist priest Father Coughlin, the anti-capitalist, anti-communist, anti-Semitic founder of the National Union for Social Justice in 1934 and of the paper Social Justice two years later, who became an apologist for Nazism and an Axis propagandist). The entire history of the twentieth century, to stick just with recent times, tells us how dangerous a path the belief in the single-minded pursuit of "social justice" is.

3 – Marxist, Racist, LGTBQ+ & Ethnic Studies

Programs Are Being Exposed

Credit: Vern Bender.

From the Robert Leroux "Woke Madness and the University" National Association of Scholars article in the Winter of 2021:

On college and university campuses, from where it emerged, the woke ideology has become a powerful instrument of censorship, a particularly clear manifestation of the intellectual terrorism that has reigned there for about half a century. In some cases, such as at Evergreen College in the State of Washington , it even encourages violence. In fact, woke culture is the intellectual plague of our times.

We must say that what we now call the woke culture or movement is nothing new. It is part of a long tradition, influenced by Marxism, feminism, relativism, etc. It is not a scientific approach to reality, but essentially an ideological posture, an attitude, a social movement. The situation is getting worst because most academics are now activists.

35

As early as the 1980s, in his seminal book *The Closing of the American Mind*, Allan Bloom analyzed this phenomenon in its first manifestations before the word woke was coined.

It became almost impossible to question the radical orthodoxy without risking vilification, classroom disruption, loss of the confidence and respect necessary for teaching, and the hostility of colleagues. Racist and sexist were, and are, very ugly labels—the equivalents of atheist or communist in other days with other prevailing prejudices—which can be pinned on persons promiscuously and which, once attached, are almost impossible to cast off. Nothing could be said with impunity. Such an atmosphere made detached, dispassionate study impossible."

For Bloom, it became almost impossible to question extremist orthodoxy without running the risk of being vilified as an intolerant person. The situation today is not really different.

New generations of professors have been hired not because they are concerned with and dedicated to science and objective knowledge, but because they are mainly political activists. Everything is wrong with the woke ideology: extreme paranoia, a mistaken view of social life, free speech, and the common man. Listening to the doctrinaires of the woke movement, we see that we are entering an unreal world, based on exaggerations, resolutely closed to dialogue and debate.

With wokeness, we cannot have a better example of the extreme radicalization of the left.

The left, which was once devoted to the fate of the working class and its struggles belongs to a bygone past. At the University of Ottawa, on a job posting one can read this:

The Institute of Feminist and Gender Studies at the University of Ottawa, located on the traditional and unceded territory of the Anishinabe-Algonquin people, is accepting applications for one tenure-track position in Afro-feminist studies. Applications from people who work with an intersectional framework on Islamophobia and anti-black racism, solidarities between Black and Indigenous people, transnational feminisms, Black feminist methodologies and practices, queer of color or black trans studies and/or the history and impacts of slavery in Francophone contexts, are particularly welcome. Community experience is an asset, as is bilingualism . . . Qualified Black applicants from Africa or the African diaspora (descended from the Caribbean, North America, Europe, Latin America, etc.) are invited to apply for this position.

The description is ridiculous!

Wokeness views the world today with great disdain, indeed hates it bitterly. Not only must social distinctions disappear, it is, above all, important that politicized racial, sexual, and gender groups impose their interests and their vision on the world.

Like Marxism, this doctrine delivers the individual to servitude: we flout him, we censor him, we impose a new vocabulary on him, even a new way of thinking. It is clear that many universities have become liberticidal.

How Public Schools Went Woke—and What to Do About It

As per the Daniel Buck and Garion Frankel "How Public Schools Went Woke—and What to Do about It" *National Review* report in March 2022:

A radical theory of education—one that sees the classroom as the locus of societal change, not academic training—dominates our colleges of education. Thus, like a drainage pipe into a common supply, teacher-prep programs around the country dump a politicized approach to education into our schools, and it is here where our reform efforts must focus.

This outsized influence of the university on K–12 schools occurs not without precedent. Once before, our nation's dominant philosophy of education universally altered. Prior to the 20th century, American education was almost universally classical in nature—great books, grammar and rhetoric, direct teacher guidance, a healthy patriotism. However, the establishment of teacher colleges began to change that. Between 1910 and 1930, 88 normal schools—local institutions to train teachers—associated with universities and became teacher colleges.

At the most influential of these, Columbia's Teachers College, John Dewey and William Kilpatrick trained 35,000 students and wrote popular essays that influenced countless more. With such an influence, the progressive pedagogy of Dewey and Kilpatrick—which rejects liberal notions of knowledge worth knowing and direct teacher guidance to instead center a student's personal interests and exploration—supplanted classical education in American schools. The theory's association with colleges of education legitimated progressive education and so flooded American schools with proclamations of "best practices" and "expertise."

The influence of teacher colleges hasn't changed, only the theory within. Today, Teachers College, still one of the most prestigious teacher-prep programs in the country with 90,000 alumni, continues its significant role in determining what occurs in K–12 classrooms. A quick scroll through Columbia's course catalog reveals that teacher-prep programs now look toward "liberation" rather than virtue. A popular curriculum from Teachers College encourages children to read through critical-race lenses and acknowledges its dependence on critical race theory.

The college offers a class in "Black, Latina, and Transnational Feminisms," which seeks to "engage in an interdisciplinary exploration of feminist scholarship located at the intersections of race, class, and culture." In addition, the school offers a class in "Anti-Racist Curriculum, Pedagogy, Leadership and Policy." This trend continues across the college's course offerings, with frequent mentions of gender, race, class, and inclusivity.

Notably, course descriptions rarely if ever mention instruction, curriculum, assessment, or anything having to do with educating children. It amounts to a program in "proper" political opinions, not the practicalities of classroom instruction.

And Teachers College Is No Outlier

An education-policy course at the also influential University of Wisconsin-Madison "[focuses] on the ideas of transformative educators such as Paulo Freire and bell hooks (and yes, her name is all lower case!)." Freire's *Pedagogy of the Oppressed*, an incoherent attempt to explore the parasitic relationship between oppressor and oppressed in the context of the classroom, is considered a seminal work by many teacher-prep programs. References to Freire and other advocates of critical pedagogy appear on the syllabi of Harvard, UC Berkeley, California State-Long Beach, and the University of North Texas.

A UW professor, Gloria Ladson-Billings, is considered one of the single most influential thinkers in education. In 1998, she synthesized CRT and K–12 education, and in 2021, Indianapolis Public Schools hosted her at a racial-equity training for teachers.

Simply look through the DEI offerings at local schools to see that references to Freire, Billings, hooks, and other radical theorists abound. The organization Teachers Without Borders encourages their educators to understand and implement Freire's theory of "peace education"—ironic, considering that Freire cites Che Guevara and Lenin as exemplary teachers. After the passing of bell hooks in 2021, countless testimonials appeared online of how teachers implemented her ideas in their classrooms.

Woke ideas about race and power did not form ex nihilo in the minds of DEI consultants at K–12 schools. They stem from a decades-long process that saw a noteworthy shift in the research interests of education faculty. As the DEI fad caught on, its teachings made their way to both university and K–12 classrooms. Moreover, the transformation of the university's pedagogical environment is not an unprecedented event. Once again, Columbia and universities like it are acting like a superspreader event of critical pedagogy and other radical ideas.

That our teaching force requires their credentials ensures that the drainage pipe will flow on. Even if we ban explicit instruction in something like CRT, its ideas can still influence policy, curricula, behavior plans, and teaching. Even if school-choice bills passed in every state today, the same teaching force trained in the precepts of Freire and other pedagogues would staff our schools tomorrow. We must decouple the colleges of education and schools by ending teacher-licensing requirements.

Thankfully, schools don't seem to need these schools of education. Research into the efficacy of such programs finds "little difference in the average academic achievement impacts of certified, uncertified and alternatively certified teachers." More like a degree in business than medicine, official teacher-training may assist in initial hiring but is no guarantee of effectiveness. In fact, many successful charter schools run on a model that relies on well-educated but untrained recent graduates who then undergo rigorous on-the-job training and constant professional development.

There are other potential knock-on benefits of ending our licensing racket. Burdensome processes that require years of training and financial investment create an opportunity cost that dissuades talented would-be candidates from other professions. Furthermore, fewer regulatory hoops to jump through could encourage entry into the profession and thereby mitigate the teacher-shortage crisis that our schools currently face.

Any attempt at reform—reestablishing classical and liberal conceptions of education in these institutions—would take a 50-year Gramscian countermarch of our universities. As such, our only recourse is to sever the control they have over teacher training.

CRT: The Monster Is in the Classroom

Per the Erika Sanzi "The Monster Is in the Classroom" *City Journal* report in April 2021:

Many American parents may assume that culture-war battles over critical race theory and "wokeness" are fought on legitimate terrain, involving such matters as how high school students can best grapple with our nation's complex past. Perhaps they think that the suddenly ubiquitous topics of gender identity and preferred pronouns rankle only those parents who are old-fashioned in their thinking. If only. America's youngest students are being bombarded with classroom activism and indoctrination that is inappropriate not only developmentally but for public school systems in general.

The contemporary obsession with identity has made its way into elementary school policy, curricula, and standards approved by state boards. While we continue to see poor reading and math scores, schools spend money and time confusing and shaming other people's children. Many educators and elected leaders have good intentions; they believe deeply that they are part of a necessary and long-overdue movement to teach racial literacy, social justice, equity, and antiracism.

But as virtuous as these terms may sound on their face, they mean something else in far too many classrooms. American schools are teaching young children race essentialism: reducing them to identity groups, putting them in boxes labeled "oppressor" and "oppressed," and often inflicting emotional and psychological harm.

If This Sounds Extreme, That's Because It Is

Schools indoctrinate children as young as eight in race and gender essentialism.

It is not happening everywhere—but it is happening enough to have juiced a multibillion-dollar, nationwide industry. Sometimes the source is a rogue teacher whom the principal and superintendent admit they are trying to rein in; but increasingly, it is simply public officials implementing approved policies.

- Consider Bellevue, Washington, home to Cherry Crest Elementary School. The school website indicates that students "will have explicit conversations about race, equity, and access" and "will identify culture and begin to recognize and identify white culture through storytelling, sharing, and conversation." The school promises to hold monthly assemblies that focus on culture, identity, and race, and has created a group called SOAR (Students Organized Against Racism) for fourth- and fifth-graders. These children, who range from ages nine to 11, are tasked with "implementing learning and stratimplementation of school-wide learning and strategies for being anti-racist." Left unclear is whether these students have been made aware that modern antiracism requires discrimination on the basis of race.

- Or take Lexington, Massachusetts, where, in October 2019, fourth-graders were taught to "articulate what gender identity is and why it's important to use nonbinary language in describing people we don't know yet." According to photos shared on Twitter by the district's Director of Equity and Student Supports, students learned about "gender identity," "gender expression," "sexual orientation," and "sex assigned at birth" by examining sticky notes on a "Gender Snowperson" who was drawn in magic marker on a large sheet of paper. The students were also taught that their pronouns had been "assigned at birth."

- In Oregon, teachers can use new state standards in "ethnic studies" starting in September 2021; the standards will become a mandatory part of the curriculum in 2025. The Oregon Department of Education released an update on the standards in 2020. While most Americans may not consider gender an essential component of ethnic studies, the Oregon Department of Education does. The revised recommendations for the standards require kindergartners to "understand their own identity groups, including but not limited to race, gender, family, ethnicity, culture, religion and ability." First-graders will be able to "describe how individual and group characteristics are used to divide, unite, and categorize racial, ethnic and social groups."

- In Rockwood, Missouri, a fifth-grade teacher recently gave students a handout with written excerpts by Alicia Garza, co-founder of Black Lives Matter. The writings included the claim that

41

"Michael Brown was murdered just steps from his mother's home in Ferguson, Missouri." (They did not mention Attorney General Eric Holder's conclusion that "the facts did not support the filing of criminal charges against Officer Darren Wilson.") The handout goes on: "Disruption is the new world order. It is the way in which those denied power assert power. And in the context of a larger strategy for how to contend for power, disruption is an important way to surface new possibilities." When I asked the school principal about the assignment, he said: "This was used by a teacher and is not a Rockwood approved resource. I am working with the teacher to ensure that only Rockwood curricular resources are used when teaching lessons."

- This past February 2021, students in Evanston, Illinois, listened to the book *Not My Idea: A Book About Whiteness*. Parents were asked to discuss the book with their children at home. The book says that "whiteness is a bad deal" and "always was," and that "you can be white without signing on to whiteness." As Conor Friedersdorf reports in *The Atlantic*, Evanston schools ask kindergarten parents to quiz their five- and six-year-olds on whiteness and to give them examples of "how whiteness shows up in school or in the community."

- In Cupertino, California, third-graders at R. I. Meyerholz Elementary School were required to deconstruct their racial identities and then rank themselves according to their "power and privilege." The teacher asked all students to create an "identity map," which required them to list their race, class, gender, religion, family structure, and other characteristics. The teacher explained to students that they live in a "dominant culture" of "white, middle class, cisgender, educated, able-bodied, Christian, English speaker[s]," who, according to the lesson, "created and maintained" this culture in order "to hold power and stay in power." Students were then asked to deconstruct these intersectional identities and "circle the identities that hold power and privilege" on their identity maps, ranking their traits based on the hierarchy the teacher had just explained to them.

Some parents may agree with such content. But public institutions funded with public dollars do not exist to groom activists for particular causes, shame children for their immutable traits, or deny them their agency or

42

their childhood. We are talking about eight- and nine-year-old kids who believe in Santa Claus, hide their lost teeth under their pillow for the tooth fairy, and curl up in their parents' laps for comfort and love. It is immoral—at least—to reduce them to confected racial and gender categories and to teach them to do the same to others. Parents around the country need to understand what is happening in a growing number of elementary classrooms.

"Banging Beyond Binaries"

Per the Christopher F. Rufo "Banging Beyond Binaries" *City Journal* article in May 2022:

In early July 2021, the district's Office of Diversity, Equity, and Inclusion sent invitations to the Philadelphia Trans Wellness Conference to teachers and staff on the SDP Connect mailing list, promoting the conference as a way to "learn more about the issues facing the trans community." The School District of Philadelphia encouraged teachers to attend a conference on "kink," "BDSM," "trans sex," and "banging beyond binaries."

The conference was organized by the Mazzoni Center, an LGBTQ activist organization that has worked with the district on sexual-education programs. (When reached for comment, the School District of Philadelphia described its promotion of the conference as part of its commitment to "creating equitable and inclusive environments," and said it did "not have any information" on the number of teachers who attended the event. The Mazzoni Center did not return request for comment.)

I have obtained videos from a publicly accessible website that show that the conference went far beyond the school district's euphemism about "issues facing the trans community." The event included sessions on topics such as "The Adolescent Pathway: Preparing Young People for Gender-Affirming Care," "Bigger Dick Energy: Life After Masculinizing [Gender Reassignment Surgery]," "Prosthetics for Sex," "The Ins and Outs of Masturbation Sleeves," and "Trans Sex: Banging Beyond Binaries."

The conference attendees included educators, activists, adults, and adolescents. There were graphic sessions on prosthetic penises, masturbation toys, and artificial ejaculation devices, which some hosts explicitly promoted to minors. As one session host explained, "there's no age limit, because I feel like everybody should be able to access certain information."

The conference began with presentations promoting puberty blockers, hormone treatments, breast removals, and genital surgeries. In one session, "The Adolescent Pathway Preparing Young People for Gender-Affirming Care," Dr. Scott Mosser, the principal at the Gender Confirmation Center in San Francisco, explained that he has performed "over two thousand top surgeries," which involve removing girls' breasts, and that there is no age limit for beginning the "gender journey."

"I do not have a minimum age of any sort in my practice," he said, explaining that he would be willing to consult with children as young as ten years old with parental consent. In another session open to children, "Gender-Affirming Masculine and Feminizing Hormones for Adolescents and Adults," Dane Menkin, divisional director of LGBTQ services at Main Line Health, endorsed treatments ranging from puberty-blocking hormones to manual breast-binding for "masculinizing" adolescent girls. "I'm a strong proponent that you can bind for as many hours a day as you can tolerate binding," he said.

Other presentations at the Trans Wellness Conference involved explicit sexual themes.

Two female-to-male trans activists, Kofi Opam, a graduate student at the University of Iowa, and Sami Brussels, a medical illustrator, hosted a presentation called "Bigger Dick Energy," in which they explained the process of phalloplasty and using an artificial penis for "navigating cruising and anonymous/casual sex life."

Chase Ross, a transgender activist and YouTuber, hosted a series of sessions on "packers," "masturbation sleeves," and "prosthetics for sex," demonstrating various devices from his collection of more than 500 genital prosthetics. "I have tried and touched many dicks, right—prosthetics, real dicks, all dicks. This is one of the most realistic feeling in terms of like the inside of a penis," he said during one demonstration. "It's a big boy, this is, like, gigantic. Alright, give me two hours alone and I'll get this in my butt," he said during another.

The most extreme presentation at the three-day conference was "Trans Sex: Banging Beyond Binaries." Jamie Joy, a self-described "kinky," "polyamorous," "pretty big slut," and Lucie Fielding, a self-described "white, queer, kinky, polyamorous, visibly able-bodied, Jewish, witchy, non-binary, trans femme" led the session.

The women led a presentation on politically correct anatomical language, including terms such as "front hole" and "back hole," and shared personal information about organizing orgies for participants to "explore their fantasies and their perversions in groups." The instructors then discussed various "kink" activities, including fetishes about puppies, Mary Poppins, and spanking. "I haven't gotten to explore a lot of my mommy kink. And I think for tonight I'm really wanting to feel cared for, but also get punished a little bit," said Joy.

It is important to remember that this conference is not a fringe activity.

The Mazzoni Center, which organized it, received more than $5 million in government contracts in 2021 and runs sexuality programs in schools throughout the region. The School District of Philadelphia has partnered with the Center on sexual-health research and student sexual-education programs, and the district's director of teacher leadership, Amy Summa, sits on Mazzoni's board of directors. Despite the school district's euphemisms about "wellness" and "self-esteem," the conference materials reveal a sexual ideology steeped in radical queer theory, not commonsense sex education. Parents and taxpayers should ask why the district's Office of Diversity, Equity, and Inclusion encouraged teachers to participate in such programming.

Radical Gender Lessons for Young Children

From the Christopher F. Rufo "Radical Gender Lessons for Young Children" *City Journal* article in April 2022:

Evanston–Skokie School District 65 has adopted a radical gender curriculum that teaches pre-kindergarten through third-grade students to celebrate the transgender flag, break the "gender binary" established by white "colonizers," and experiment with neo-pronouns such as "ze," "zir," and "tree.

Rufo has obtained the full curriculum documents, which are part of the Chicago-area district's "LGBTQ+ Equity Week," which administrators adopted in 2021. The curriculum begins in pre-kindergarten, with a series of lessons on sexual orientation and gender identity. The lesson plan opens with an introduction to the rainbow flag and teaches students that "Each color in the flag has a meaning."

The teacher also presents the transgender flag and the basic concepts of gender identity, explaining that "we call people with more than one gender or no gender, non-binary or queer." Finally, the lesson plan has the teacher leading a class project to create a rainbow flag, with instructions to "gather students on the rug," "ask them to show you their flags," and "proudly hang the class flag where they can all see it."

In kindergarten, the lessons on gender and trans identity go deeper.

"When we show whether we feel like a boy or a girl or some of each, we are expressing our GENDER IDENTITY," the lesson begins. "There are also children who feel like a girl AND a boy; or like neither a boy OR a girl. We can call these children TRANSGENDER."

Students are expected to be able to "explain the importance of the rainbow flag and trans flag" and are asked to consider their own gender identity.

The kindergartners read two books that affirm transgender conversions, study photographs of boys in dresses, learn details about the transgender flag, and perform a rainbow dance. At the end of the lesson, the students are encouraged to adopt and share their own gender identities with the class. "Now you have a chance to make a picture to show how YOU identify," the lesson reads. "Maybe you want to have blue hair! Maybe you want to be wearing a necklace. Your identity is for YOU to decide!"

In first grade, students learn about gender pronouns.

The teachers explain that "some pronouns are gender neutral" and students can adopt pronouns such as "she," "tree," "they," "he," "her," "him," "them," "ze," and "zir."

The students practice reading a series of scripts in which they announce their gender pronouns and practice using alternate pronouns, including "they," "tree," "ze," and "zir." The teacher encourages students to experiment and reminds them: "Whatever pronouns you pick today, you can always change!" Students then sit down to complete a pronouns workbook, with more lessons on neo-pronouns and non-binary identities.

In third grade, Evanston–Skokie students are told that white European "colonizers" imposed their "Western and Christian ideological framework" on racial minorities and "forced two-spirit people to conform to the gender binary."

The teacher tells students that "many people feel like they aren't really a boy or a girl" and that they should "call people by the gender they have in their heart." Students are encouraged to "break the binary," reject the system of "whiteness," and study photographs of black men in dresses and a man wearing lipstick and long earrings.

"It is a myth that gender is binary," the lesson explains.

"Even though we are all given a sex assigned at birth, you are NOT given your gender. Only you can know your gender and how you feel inside." At the end of the lesson, students are instructed to write a letter to the future on how they can change society. "Society right now is very unfair," reads a sample letter. "I see a lot of marches on the T.V. and I even went to a march last summer."

The curriculum in Evanston–Skokie School District 65 is the perfect illustration of college-level queer theory translated into early-elementary pedagogy. For weeks, as the nation has debated Florida's Parental Rights in Education Act, which prohibits public schools from teaching gender identity and sexual orientation in grades K–3, commentators on the political left have claimed that public schools do not teach this material and have accused conservatives of instigating a "moral panic."

This claim is demonstrably false, and the Evanston–Skokie lesson plans offer additional proof for parents and legislators concerned about gender ideology in American public schools. Queer theory has made its way into public school curriculums for children as young as four. This development should be subject to robust political debate, not denial and dismissal from the political Left.

Sexual Liberation in Public Schools

Per the Christopher F. Rufo "Sexual Liberation in Public Schools" *City Journal* article in July 2022:

Los Angeles Unified School District has adopted a radical gender-theory curriculum encouraging teachers to work toward the "breakdown of the gender binary," to experiment with gender pronouns such as "they," "ze," and "tree," and to adopt "trans-affirming" programming to make their classrooms "queer all school year."

Rufo has obtained a trove of publicly accessible documents from Los Angeles Unified that illustrates the extent to which gender ideology has entered the mainstream of the nation's second-largest school district. Since 2020, the district's Human Relations, Diversity, and Equity department has created an infrastructure to translate the basic tenets of academic queer theory into K-12 pedagogy. The materials include a wide range of conferences, presentations, curricula, teacher-training programs, adult-driven "gender and sexuality" clubs, and school-sponsored protests.

In a week-long conference last fall, titled "Standing with LGBTQ+ Students, Staff, and Families," administrators hosted workshops with presentations on "breaking the [gender] binary," providing children with "free gender affirming clothing," understanding "what your queer middle schooler wants you to know," and producing "counter narratives against the master narrative of mainstream white cis-heteropatriarchy society."

The narrative follows the standard academic slop: white, cisgender, heterosexual men have built a repressive social structure, divided the world into the false binary of man and woman, and used this myth to oppress racial and sexual minorities. Religion, too, is a mechanism of repression. During the conference, the district highlighted how teachers can "respond to religious objections" to gender ideology and promoted materials on how students can be "Muslim and Trans."

In another training program, titled "Queering Culture & Race," the Human Relations, Diversity, and Equity office encouraged teachers to adopt the principle of intersectionality, a key tenet of critical race theory, and apply it to the classroom.

First, administrators asked teachers to identify themselves by race, gender, and sexual orientation, and to consider their position on the identity hierarchy. The district then encouraged teachers to "avoid gendered expressions" in the classroom, including "boys and girls" and "ladies and gentlemen," which, according to queer theory, are vestiges of the oppressive gender binary.

Administrators also warned teachers that they might have to work against the families of their minority students, especially black students, regarding sexuality. "The Black community often holds rigid and traditional views of sexual orientation and gender expression," the presenters claimed. "Black LGBTQ youth experience homophobia and transphobia from their familial communities."

Finally, Los Angeles Unified has gone all-in on "trans-affirming" indoctrination.

The Human Relations, Diversity, and Equity department has flooded the district with teaching materials, including, for example, videos from the consulting firm Woke Kindergarten encouraging five-year-olds to experiment with gender pronouns such as "they," "ze," and "tree" and to adopt nonbinary gender identities that "feel good to you." The district requires teachers to use a student's desired name and pronoun and to keep the student's gender identity a secret from parents if the student so desires.

In other words, Los Angeles public schools can facilitate a child's transition from one gender to another without notifying parents. And the district is far from neutral: it actively celebrates sexual identities such as "pansexual," "sexually fluid," "queer," "same-gender-loving," and "asexual," and gender identities such as "transgender," "genderqueer," "agender," "bigender," "gender nonconforming," "gender expansive," "gender fluid," and "two-spirit."

The problem with creating a "trans-affirming" culture is obvious.

In one of the district's own materials, "Mental Health Among Transgender Youth," the Human Relations, Diversity, and Equity department cites a survey by Mental Health America pointing out that, among 11-to-17-year-old transgender youth who were screened for mental health issues, 93 percent were at risk for psychosis, 91 percent exhibited signs of posttraumatic stress disorder, 90 percent likely used drugs and alcohol, 90 percent experienced moderate-to-severe anxiety, and 95 percent experienced moderate to severe depression. Additionally, according to a Trevor Project study, 71 percent of transgender youth have been diagnosed with eating disorders, with the ratio even higher for female-to-male transgender children.

These numbers are deeply alarming. But rather than provide a sober assessment of these risks and seek to mitigate them, Los Angeles Unified has adopted a year-round program glamorizing transgender identity and promoting an uncritical, "trans-affirming" culture in the classroom. It is, of course, a noble goal for schools to provide a safe environment for minority groups and to affirm the basic dignity of all children regardless of their sexuality. But Los Angeles Unified's program goes much further, promoting the most extreme strains of transgender ideology, which almost certainly

49

contributes to the "social contagion" effect documented by Abigail Shrier and others.

The Los Angeles Unified School District governs the educational life of more than 600,000 children, the majority of whom are racial minorities from poor families. The implicit cynicism of the district's gender-ideology instruction is sickening: highly educated, well-paid bureaucrats promote fashionable academic programming that will do nothing to provide a basic education for these children or help them move up the economic and social ladder. It will only keep them trapped in a morass of confusion, fatalism, and resentment—while the bureaucrats keep collecting their paychecks.

4 – The Dangers of Forced Conformity in Diversity, Equity & Inclusion

Credit: Global Watchdog.

This chapter is from the Alan Wood "DEI Exposed: The Dangers of Forced Conformity in Diversity Equity & Inclusion" Global Watchdog March 2024 article:

Musings of an unabashed and unapologetic liberal deep in the heart of a Red State. Crusader against obscurantism. Optimistic curmudgeon, snark jockey, lovably opinionated purveyor of wisdom and truth. Multi-lingual world traveler and part-time irreverent philosopher who dabbles in writing, political analysis, and social commentary. Attempting to provide some sanity and clarity to complex issues with a dash of sardonic wit and humor. Thanks for visiting!

Beyond the Buzzwords: Unveiling the Dark Side of DEI

The mantra of Diversity, Equity, and Inclusion (DEI) has pervaded our workplaces, posing as a beacon of progress and inclusivity. Yet, beneath this polished veneer, there lies a troubling reality: systemic barriers remain entrenched, minority voices are drowned out, and a sense of disillusionment spreads like wildfire across both majority and minority groups. This stark contradiction between the lofty ideals and the sobering reality of DEI demands a rigorous, unflinching examination.

Our journey through this article is not merely academic. We are here to unravel the intricate web of economic, legal, psychological, and ethical threads that DEI initiatives weave, often to their own detriment. While the pursuit of inclusivity is noble, the path trodden by current DEI programs is fraught with pitfalls and paradoxes, leading us astray from our shared goal of a truly inclusive society.

In this critical exploration, we will lay bare the hidden dangers of DEI, dissecting its economic, legal, and psychological implications, and challenging the often-unquestioned assumptions it carries. Our aim is not to dismantle the desire for positive change but to shine a light on the chasm between aspiration and reality, igniting a necessary dialogue for genuine, effective inclusivity.

Our analysis is not just an academic exercise; it's a call to action. We stand at a crossroads, where the choice is ours to either continue down a path of superficial gestures or to pave a new way forward, rooted in substance, critical thinking, and true inclusivity. Join us as we delve into the complexities of DEI, not to dwell on its flaws but to forge a path toward a future where diversity is not just a buzzword, but a lived reality.

Through this comprehensive analysis, we will:

- **Expose the potential pitfalls and unintended consequences of current DEI initiatives.**

- **Explore the economic, legal, psychological, and ethical implications of DEI programs.**

- **Challenge the assumptions often associated with DEI and offer alternative perspectives.**

- **Promote a more nuanced and data-driven approach to fostering genuine inclusivity.**

- **Ultimately, ignite a call to action for a recalibration of DEI efforts, ensuring they align with their true purpose.**

This journey into the complexities of DEI is not about dwelling on the shortcomings of the present, but rather about laying the groundwork for a more equitable and inclusive future. It is a call for collective action, a shared responsibility to bridge the gap between intention and impact, and a commitment to building a world where diversity is not just celebrated, but truly lived and experienced by all.

Historical Context: Unveiling the Dark Side of DEI

Initially conceived as a beacon of hope against historical inequalities, DEI initiatives in academia promised inclusive environments where marginalized voices could resonate. However, the trajectory of these initiatives has veered sharply, morphing into ideological battlegrounds, as aptly observed by Fareed Zakaria. Universities, once the bastions of intellectual freedom, now find themselves ensnared in a web of ideological conformity, often at the behest of DEI advocates.

The University of Chicago's Kalven Report, a seminal document underscoring the importance of ideological neutrality in academia, seems a distant memory in today's DEI landscape. The report's call for academic freedom and open inquiry stands in stark contrast to the current state of affairs, where dissenting voices are stifled, and ideological alignment is often enforced.

This ideological drift in DEI initiatives is not just a matter of academic concern; it reflects a broader societal shift. What began as an earnest effort to rectify past injustices has, in some cases, evolved into a tool for enforcing conformity. This trend raises alarm bells, signaling a need for urgent reform to reclaim the original vision of DEI – one that truly fosters diversity of thought and promotes a pluralistic society.

Legal Risks and Compliance Challenges in DEI Programs

The legal landscape surrounding Diversity, Equity, and Inclusion (DEI) initiatives presents a complex and often overlooked aspect of these programs. As highlighted in the Reuters article by Sarah E. Fortt, Danielle Conley, and Nineveh Alkhas, "Diversity matters: the four scary legal risks hiding in your DEI program," DEI initiatives, while well-intentioned, can inadvertently lead to significant legal challenges. The authors caution, "In the rush to implement DEI initiatives, many companies overlook the importance of legal oversight, leading to potential legal actions against them."

One of the primary legal risks associated with DEI programs is non-compliance with existing anti-discrimination laws. While aiming to foster diversity, these initiatives can sometimes inadvertently create scenarios where discrimination occurs in reverse – favoring one group over another based on characteristics such as race, gender, or ethnicity. This can lead to legal challenges, as the authors note: "DEI goals, especially when poorly framed, can sometimes clash with the legal framework designed to prevent discrimination."

Moreover, the implementation of DEI programs often lacks a comprehensive understanding of regulatory requirements, leading to a mismatch between the initiatives and the legal framework within which organizations operate. This gap can expose organizations to legal risks, as Fortt, Conley, and Alkhas warn, "Failure to consider all stakeholders and regulatory requirements can lead to initiatives that are more harmful than helpful."

Another article, "7 Ways Your DEI Initiatives Are Harming Your Company and How To Resolve It" by Brian Dapelo, echoes similar concerns, highlighting how DEI programs can inadvertently lead to workplace discrimination. Dapelo states, "In their quest for diversity, some organizations end up discriminating in the name of inclusion, paradoxically undermining the very principles DEI stands for."

Furthermore, DEI initiatives sometimes lack sufficient legal support, particularly for DEI officers tasked with implementing these programs. This oversight can result in a disjointed approach that fails to align DEI efforts with legal and regulatory standards, as noted in the Reuters article: "Insufficient legal support for DEI officers can lead to initiatives that are legally unsound and potentially damaging."

These legal and compliance challenges underscore the necessity for a more cautious and legally informed approach to DEI initiatives. As organizations strive to create inclusive environments, they must navigate the complex legal landscape with care, ensuring that their efforts to promote diversity do not inadvertently lead to new forms of discrimination or legal entanglements.

Effectiveness and Counterproductivity of DEI Training

The effectiveness and potential counterproductivity of Diversity, Equity, and Inclusion (DEI) training programs have been a subject of intense debate. Rod Dreher, in his article "DEI Training: Harmful, Phony, And Expensive" published by The American Conservative, presents a critical view, arguing that these programs are costly, ineffective, and may even reinforce biases. He cites research suggesting that "DEI training is a high-cost endeavor with little evidence of long-term effectiveness."

Dreher further criticizes the approach of DEI training, often seen as performative rather than transformative. He notes that "instead of fostering genuine understanding, DEI training can provoke backlash and deepen divisions." This sentiment resonates with other critiques questioning the focus on personal belief changes, a strategy deemed both intrusive and ineffective. The simplistic view of complex social dynamics adopted by some DEI training programs is also highlighted as problematic. As Dreher points out, "DEI training oversimplifies the complexities of human behavior and interaction, leading to superficial solutions to deep-rooted problems."

These criticisms raise concerns about a potential disconnect between the goals of DEI training and its real-world impact. Instead of fostering inclusivity and understanding, some programs may actually contribute to division and skepticism about their value and efficacy.

Misguided Focus and Unintended Outcomes of DEI Initiatives

While intended to promote workplace and societal harmony, Diversity, Equity, and Inclusion (DEI) initiatives can ironically lead to various unintended and adverse consequences. This section draws on Brian Dapelo's analysis in "7 Ways Your DEI Initiatives Are Harming Your Company and How To Resolve It," which outlines several critical concerns.

Dapelo highlights the potential for DEI efforts to inadvertently promote discrimination. He argues that "flawed execution can result in favoring certain groups over others, contradicting the principles of equality and fairness." This can create resentment and undermine the very goals of DEI initiatives.

Furthermore, the overemphasis on physical attributes in some DEI programs, instead of focusing on individual qualities and merit, is another concern. Dapelo warns that "such practices can diminish the overall talent pool and decrease performance by prioritizing external characteristics over skills and experience." This not only undermines meritocratic principles but can also foster divisiveness within organizations.

Additionally, attributing individual accomplishments to demographic factors rather than personal merit can be demotivating and counterproductive. Dapelo observes that "such practices can belittle individual achievements, creating a workplace culture that prioritizes labels over individual contributions."

Finally, the potential for DEI initiatives to distract from core organizational goals is another critical point. Dapelo notes that "an excessive focus on DEI can lead to a dilution of focus and resources, hindering the achievement of primary objectives."

These critiques raise serious questions about the effectiveness of conventional DEI approaches. While the intentions behind such programs are often commendable, their implementation can lead to outcomes that are directly counterproductive to the goals of fairness and inclusivity. The following section will delve deeper into the systemic issues associated with these conventional approaches and explore alternative solutions.

Systemic Issues and Superficial Approaches in Conventional DEI Initiatives

While Diversity, Equity, and Inclusion (DEI) initiatives are intended to create inclusive environments and address historical inequalities, they often face criticism for their systemic issues and superficial approaches. Dr. Ted Sun, in his article "Dangers of the Conventional DEI Initiatives," published by Transcontinental University, delves into these concerns.

Sun argues that traditional DEI training can be ineffective and even harmful. He describes a "blame game" within such programs, which fails to foster genuine understanding or lasting change. Furthermore, he criticizes quota-driven approaches, a common feature in DEI initiatives, suggesting that they prioritize superficial diversity without addressing underlying biases or building meaningful relationships across diverse groups.

Sun advocates for a shift towards a values-based systemic approach to DEI. This approach emphasizes core values awareness and leadership development, aiming to move beyond the limitations of quotas and training. By addressing unconscious bias at a deeper level, it seeks to create lasting change and build a truly inclusive culture. Sun warns that without a values-driven foundation, DEI initiatives risk becoming counterproductive, exacerbating the very divisions they are meant to bridge.

This critique emphasizes the need for a more holistic and value-centric approach to diversity and inclusion. One that goes beyond superficial measures and integrates into the very fabric of organizational culture, promoting genuine understanding and respect for all individuals.

Comprehensive Analysis and Case Studies on the Dangers of DEI Initiatives

This section delves into the dangers of Diversity, Equity, and Inclusion (DEI) initiatives through a series of case studies and expanded critiques, providing a comprehensive picture of the challenges these programs often encounter.

Case Study 1: Impingement on Free Speech and Open Debate

In Fareed Zakaria's article, he details a case from a U.S. university where events organized by Students for Justice in Palestine were disrupted. This incident illustrates how DEI efforts, despite good intentions, can inadvertently stifle free speech and open debate in academic settings. The delicate balance between promoting inclusivity and preserving the bedrock principles of academic freedom and dialogue is a challenge DEI initiatives often struggle to navigate.

Case Study 2: Legal Ramifications and Reverse Discrimination

An article from Reuters discusses a situation where a corporate DEI initiative led to a lawsuit alleging reverse discrimination. This example highlights the potential legal risks associated with DEI programs and emphasizes the need for meticulous legal oversight in their implementation. Balancing the goal of fostering diversity and inclusion with adhering to legal and ethical standards presents a significant challenge for organizations.

Case Study 3: Unintended Reinforcement of Biases

Rod Dreher critiques corporate DEI training in his article, highlighting a case where training sessions inadvertently reinforced existing biases rather than diminishing them. This demonstrates the potential for DEI training to backfire, exacerbating the very problems it seeks to resolve and heightening workplace tensions.

Case Study 4: Decreased Performance and Increased Divisiveness

Brian Dapelo analyzes a company where DEI initiatives led to decreased overall performance and increased employee divisiveness. This example illustrates the potential for poorly managed DEI efforts to be counterproductive, dividing the workforce instead of unifying it.

Case Study 5: Superficial Diversity Efforts

Dr. Ted Sun's analysis focuses on an organization that prioritized meeting diversity quotas without addressing underlying systemic issues. This well-intentioned approach resulted in a veneer of diversity that failed to create a truly inclusive or equitable environment. It serves as a reminder that DEI initiatives must delve beyond superficial changes to effect real, systemic transformation.

Beyond Specific Examples: Broader Considerations

In addition to these specific cases, we also explore the broader impacts of DEI initiatives, including their psychological effects on individuals, economic implications for organizations, and long-term efficacy in achieving societal change. The global dimension of DEI is also considered, emphasizing the need for culturally nuanced approaches. This analysis of DEI initiatives, through diverse perspectives and real-world examples, highlights the complexity of these programs and the multifaceted challenges they face. By acknowledging these challenges and implementing thoughtful, nuanced, and well-executed strategies, DEI can contribute positively to organizations and society as a whole.

Alternative Approaches and Solutions

In light of the limitations of conventional Diversity, Equity, and Inclusion (DEI) initiatives, exploring alternative approaches that foster genuine inclusivity and effectiveness becomes crucial. This section delves into several promising solutions.

Values-Based Systemic Approach:

Dr. Ted Sun proposes a critical shift from quota-driven methods to a values-based systemic approach. This approach prioritizes integrating core values and leadership development into DEI strategies, aiming to address unconscious bias and build authentic relationships within organizations. This shift fosters a culture of inclusivity and respect, rather than solely focusing on numerical representation.

Promoting Inclusive Actions and Behaviors:

Instead of attempting to change personal beliefs, a more practical and effective approach focuses on promoting inclusive actions and behaviors. This involves creating environments where diverse perspectives are not only included but also valued and respected, nurturing a genuinely inclusive atmosphere where everyone feels comfortable contributing their unique experiences and perspectives.

Legal and Compliance Integration:

Ensuring that DEI initiatives comply with legal and ethical standards is crucial. This necessitates close collaboration with legal teams to design programs that adhere to anti-discrimination laws and other relevant regulations. By prioritizing legal and ethical compliance, organizations can safeguard themselves against potential legal pitfalls while promoting fairness and equity.

Cultural Competence Training:

Generic DEI training often falls short, failing to address the nuances of cultural differences. Culturally competent training, however, focuses on enhancing understanding and respect for diverse cultural backgrounds. This becomes especially crucial in a globalized workforce where cultural misunderstandings can lead to conflict and exclusion. Cultivating cultural competence is essential for building a truly inclusive environment.

Long-Term Commitment and Continuous Evaluation:

Viewing DEI initiatives as a long-term commitment rather than a one-off effort is vital for their success. Regularly measuring the impact and effectiveness of these programs through surveys, data analysis, and feedback mechanisms is essential to ensure they are achieving their intended goals and making a real difference. This commitment to ongoing evaluation and improvement underscores the importance of sustainability and adaptability in DEI initiatives.

By adopting these alternative approaches, organizations and institutions can create DEI initiatives that are legally sound, ethically robust, and truly effective in fostering diversity, equity, and inclusion. A strategic shift towards values-driven, culturally competent, and adaptable DEI strategies is imperative for realizing the full potential of diversity in our society.

Equity vs. Equality in DEI Initiatives

A critical analysis of Diversity, Equity, and Inclusion (DEI) initiatives reveals a crucial distinction between two key concepts: equity and equality. While often used interchangeably, these terms have vastly different implications for DEI efforts.

Defining the Difference:

- **Equality:** Providing every individual with the same resources and opportunities, regardless of their background or circumstances.

- **Equity:** Recognizing and addressing the individual and systemic challenges faced by different groups, ensuring everyone has equal opportunities to succeed.

The Pitfalls of Overemphasizing Equality:

Many DEI initiatives prioritize treating everyone the same, overlooking the unique needs and barriers faced by diverse groups. This approach falls short by failing to address the root causes of inequality. For example, offering identical training to all employees ignores the fact that some may require additional support or specialized resources to overcome systemic hurdles.

The Necessity of Equity-Focused DEI Initiatives:

True inclusivity necessitates a shift towards equity-focused DEI strategies. This requires acknowledging and addressing the individual and systemic challenges faced by different groups. Examples of equity-focused strategies include:

- **Targeted mentoring programs:** Supporting underrepresented groups through mentorship programs tailored to their specific needs.

- **Adjusted recruitment strategies:** Reaching a broader pool of candidates by diversifying recruitment channels and removing biased practices.

- **Accessibility measures:** Making the workplace accessible and inclusive for individuals with disabilities.

- **Culturally competent leadership:** Developing leaders who are aware of and sensitive to cultural differences.

Case Study: The Tech Industry and the Need for Equity:

The tech industry provides a compelling case study. Despite efforts to promote diversity, many underrepresented groups continue to face unique challenges that are not addressed by a one-size-fits-all approach. An equity-focused strategy, acknowledging the specific barriers faced by each group, is crucial for achieving lasting change.

Implementing Effective Equity Strategies:

Effective equity strategies require:

- **Deep understanding:** Engaging in continuous dialogue and listening to the needs of various groups.

- **Regular assessment:** Evaluating the effectiveness of current DEI strategies and identifying areas for improvement.

- **Adaptability:** Responding to feedback and adjusting strategies based on changing circumstances.

Shifting the focus from equality to equity is essential for achieving the true goals of DEI initiatives. By understanding the different needs of diverse groups and implementing tailored strategies to address them, DEI initiatives can create truly inclusive environments where everyone has the opportunity to thrive.

The Economic Dimension of DEI: Misallocation and Inefficiency

While Diversity, Equity, and Inclusion (DEI) initiatives have gained momentum, their economic impact deserves closer examination. This section explores the potential for misallocation of resources and inefficiencies within DEI programs, raising questions about their cost-effectiveness and overall impact.

Resource Allocation and Return on Investment:

A significant concern is whether the substantial financial resources directed towards DEI initiatives are translating into proportional benefits. A critical assessment of the return on investment (ROI) is needed, focusing on tangible improvements in workplace diversity, productivity, and overall organizational well-being.

Efficiency in Achieving Desired Outcomes:

The efficiency of DEI initiatives is often questioned. While significant funds are allocated to workshops, training programs, and various other activities, the effectiveness of these expenditures in achieving desired outcomes like inclusivity and equitable opportunities remains unclear. This raises the need to identify more efficient means of utilizing these resources.

Economic Impact of Misguided DEI Efforts:

Misguided or poorly implemented DEI programs can have unintended negative economic consequences. For example, initiatives that inadvertently lead to a divided workforce, reduced morale, or even legal challenges can result in significant financial losses for organizations.

Strategic and Targeted DEI Investments:

To enhance the effectiveness of DEI initiatives, a more strategic and targeted approach to resource allocation is crucial. This involves prioritizing key areas for investment, implementing evidence-based practices, and continuously evaluating the effectiveness of these interventions.

Incorporating Economic Analysis in DEI Planning:

Thorough economic analysis should be incorporated into the planning and execution of DEI initiatives. This involves setting clear, measurable goals, assessing the cost-effectiveness of different strategies, and regularly evaluating progress towards achieving these goals.

Ensuring the economic viability and effectiveness of DEI initiatives requires a strategic and data-driven approach. By prioritizing impactful interventions, utilizing resources efficiently, and continuously evaluating progress, DEI programs can achieve meaningful and sustainable progress towards diversity, equity, and inclusion while maintaining economic viability.

Cult-Like Behavior and Intellectual Stifling in DEI Initiatives

The implementation of Diversity, Equity, and Inclusion (DEI) initiatives has, in some cases, exhibited concerning trends that resemble cult-like behavior and intellectual restriction. This section explores how these issues can manifest and the negative consequences they have on open discourse and intellectual diversity.

Suppression of Dissent: A worrying trend is the suppression of dissenting voices that challenge the prevailing DEI narrative. The case of Professor Dorian Abbot at MIT, whose lecture was canceled due to his views on DEI, exemplifies this issue. Such incidents highlight how certain DEI environments become echo chambers, intolerant of diverse perspectives.

Cultish Monomania: In some cases, DEI efforts exhibit a "cultish monomania," where promoting diversity morphs into enforcing a singular, unquestionable set of beliefs. This creates an environment where any association with ideas deemed incompatible with the DEI agenda is deemed "impure" and leads to exclusion or censure.

Impact on Intellectual Discourse: This monolithic approach stifles intellectual exploration and debate. In academic settings, where diverse viewpoints and critical thinking are crucial, this trend poses a significant threat to intellectual rigor and discovery.

Monoculture of Thought: The cult-like adherence to specific DEI doctrines risks creating a monoculture of thought, where dissenting voices are not just discouraged but actively silenced. This undermines the very goals of DEI, which aim to foster inclusivity and respect for diverse perspectives.

Need for Balance: To avoid these pitfalls, a more balanced and inclusive approach is necessary. This includes creating spaces for open and respectful dialogue, where differing opinions are welcome and valued as essential components of a truly inclusive environment. DEI initiatives must resist the temptation to become dogmatic and remain open to a plurality of perspectives to be truly effective and uphold their integrity. Only through such a balanced approach can DEI foster environments that are both inclusive and intellectually vibrant.

The Illiberal Nature of DEI Initiatives

Despite their intended goals of promoting diversity and inclusion, some Diversity, Equity, and Inclusion (DEI) initiatives have been criticized for their illiberal nature, particularly concerning intellectual freedom and diversity of thought. This section examines how, paradoxically, DEI efforts can stifle dissent and create environments intolerant of differing viewpoints.

Conformity over Diversity of Thought: One key criticism is the prioritization of ideological conformity over genuine diversity of thought. This concern extends from academic institutions to corporate settings, where individuals might feel pressured to conform to specific beliefs promoted by DEI programs.

Stifling Academic and Intellectual Freedom: The potential threat to academic freedom and open discourse is particularly concerning in educational institutions. DEI initiatives that penalize individuals for holding dissenting views can significantly hinder intellectual exploration and discovery.

Creating Intellectual Echo Chambers: By fostering environments where only certain viewpoints are tolerated, DEI initiatives risk creating intellectual echo chambers. This can stifle creativity and innovation, ultimately undermining the very diversity and inclusivity these programs aim to achieve.

Balancing DEI with Intellectual Diversity: Finding the right balance between DEI goals and intellectual diversity is crucial. Effective DEI initiatives should create spaces where diverse perspectives are welcomed, encouraged, and engaged with in a respectful and constructive manner.

Encouraging Open Dialogue and Debate: Open dialogue and debate are essential for fostering a truly inclusive environment. DEI programs should provide platforms for diverse opinions to be shared and discussed without fear of retribution. This not only enriches the discourse but also promotes understanding and inclusivity. While the intentions of DEI initiatives are commendable, it is crucial to ensure that they do not become counterproductive by stifling intellectual freedom and diversity of thought. A balanced and open approach is essential for DEI initiatives to truly foster inclusive environments that embrace a broad spectrum of perspectives.

Conclusion: A Call for Recalibration and Responsible DEI

This comprehensive analysis has exposed the potential pitfalls and unintended consequences of current Diversity, Equity, and Inclusion (DEI) initiatives. While the pursuit of inclusivity is undeniably noble, the current approach, with its emphasis on superficiality, conformity, and ideological adherence, poses serious threats to fundamental freedoms and societal cohesion.

The evidence presented throughout this analysis paints a sobering picture:

- **Impingement on Free Speech and Open Debate:** DEI initiatives can inadvertently stifle open dialogue and critical discourse, creating environments of intellectual conformity.

- **Legal Ramifications and Reverse Discrimination:** Poorly designed DEI programs can lead to legal challenges and unintended consequences, undermining the very principles of fairness and equity they aim to promote.

- **Unintended Reinforcement of Biases:** Generic DEI training may inadvertently reinforce existing biases instead of dismantling them, further exacerbating societal divisions.

- **Superficial Diversity Efforts:** Focusing on quotas and superficial changes without addressing underlying systemic issues fails to create genuine inclusivity and perpetuates the feeling of tokenism.

- **Economic Misallocation and Inefficiency:** The substantial resources allocated to DEI initiatives may not be yielding proportional benefits, raising concerns about the economic viability and effectiveness of these programs.

Therefore, a call for mere reform is insufficient. A fundamental reevaluation of the entire DEI paradigm is essential. This requires a shift from:

- **Superficiality to substance:** Moving beyond tokenism and quotas to address underlying systemic issues that perpetuate inequality.

- **Conformity to diversity of thought:** Encouraging open dialogue, critical thinking, and the acceptance of diverse viewpoints.

- **Ideological adherence to merit:** Focusing on individual merit and potential rather than enforcing a specific set of beliefs.

- **Economic inefficiency to effectiveness:** Implementing cost-effective and evidence-based strategies that maximize the impact of DEI initiatives.

This recalibration of DEI efforts necessitates:

- **Critical assessment of existing initiatives:** Evaluating the effectiveness of current programs and identifying areas for improvement.

- **Development of data-driven approaches:** Utilizing evidence-based practices and setting clear, measurable goals to track progress.

- **Transparency and accountability:** Ensuring transparency in the implementation of DEI initiatives and holding organizations accountable for their outcomes.

- **Continuous dialogue and feedback:** Fostering open communication and actively seeking feedback from diverse stakeholders.

Ultimately, the goal is to create a society that embraces genuine inclusivity, respects individual dignity, and upholds the core values of equality, freedom, and meritocracy. This requires a collective effort from individuals, institutions, and organizations to move beyond the current flawed DEI paradigm and build a future where diversity is truly valued and celebrated in all its forms.

This call to action is not just about dismantling harmful practices; it is about building a better future for all. It is a chance to create a society where everyone feels welcome, valued, and empowered to contribute their unique perspectives and talents. It is time to embark on a journey towards a more inclusive, just, and equitable world.

5 – Woke Inc. and the Telos of Truth vs. Social Justice

Credit: Woke Inc. by Vivek Ramaswamy.

Our society, it seems, has failed to transmit our values, in particular free speech, to the next generation. According to a new survey by the Pew Research Center, 40 per cent of Millennials support government censorship of speech offensive to minority groups. The poll found that Millennials were the most likely of any age group to agree that government should have the authority to stop people from saying things that offend minorities.

From *The S.A.P.I.E.N.T. Being: A Critical Thinking Guide to Help Stop & Prevent Academia's Neo-Marxist & Racist Progressivist Agenda*, there can be little doubt that our society is not doing a very good job in transmitting our history and values to the next generation. A recent survey of 1,100 colleges and universities found that only eighteen percent require American history or government, where the foundations of our society, such as the First Amendment, can be explained.

The survey, by the American Council of Trustees and Alumni (ACTA), found that at the universities where free speech is now under attack, such as the University Missouri, Amherst, and Yale, very little is being done to transmit our history and values. There seems to be a correlation.

Is it any wonder that at such institutions, those in charge tend to recoil from any defense of free speech?

Measuring the Freedom of Expression Climate on Campus

Civil debate, discourse and critical thinking are perfectly consistent with an environment where people are talking *past* one-another, or *at* one-another, yet more effective when we speak *with* one-another, and work collaboratively and iteratively to understand and address difficult problems. This requires institutional norms and culture based on mutual respect—and a commitment to constructive disagreement. These cultural components cannot be effectively legislated or imposed, but they can be measured.

Simultaneously, institutional policies, procedures and incentive models of colleges and universities are changing. The needs, priorities, and expectations among new cohorts of students are evolving—even as the political climate in the United States (and beyond) has grown increasingly polarized and toxic. The result is a highly-combustible campus environment. Professors and students alike describe the toll of self-censoring and the ever-present threat of social or bureaucratic censure have taken on learning, discovery, and growth.

An effective assessment of a campuses' intellectual climate would, therefore, require an evaluation of:

1. Whether or not a school's policies protect or undermine free expression.

2. How diverse the intellectual community is, and...

3. How free students and faculty from different groups feel to share their views or express disagreement.

Americans used to frequently quote Voltaire's declaration: "I disapprove of what you say, but I will defend to the death your right to say it." This is no longer the case at too many of our colleges and universities. We have entered the era of what has been called "the heckler's veto."

Nat Hentoff, a long-time eloquent advocate for free speech, said, "First Amendment law is clear that everyone has the right to picket a speaker, and go inside a hall and heckle him or her—but not to drown out the speaker, let alone rush the stage and stop the speech before it starts. That's called the 'heckler's veto.'"

Universities Are Becoming Increasingly Hostile to Diverse Ideas

A recent study by the American Association of Colleges and Universities (AACU) of 24,000 college students and 9,000 faculty and staff members found that only eighteen per cent of the faculty and staff strongly agreed that it was "safe to hold unpopular positions on campus."

There is a difference between an opinion and an argument. An opinion is an expression of preference; it does not require any support (although it is stronger with support). An opinion is only the first part of an argument and to be complete, arguments should have three parts: an assertion, reasoning, and evidence (easily remembered with the mnemonic ARE).

We live in a climate ripe for noise: Media outlets and 24-hour news cycles mean that everyone with access to a computer has access to a megaphone to broadcast their views. Never before in human history has an opinion had the opportunity to reach so many so quickly regardless of its accuracy or appropriateness. This is a huge problem!

Educators are well positioned to provide a counterweight to this loudest-is-best approach. Speaking in a classroom or school environment is different from speaking in the outside world. Schools and classrooms strive to be safe places where students can exchange ideas, try out opinions and receive feedback on their ideas without fear or intimidation.

Children, of course, often come to school with opinions or prejudices they have learned in their homes or from the media. This means that it is also possible for schools to become places of intolerance and fear, especially for students who voice minority opinions.

Schools must work to be sites of social transformation where teachers and young people find ways to communicate effectively.

The Heckler's Veto and Squelching Speech

The sad reality is that many college campuses today have become hotbeds of bullying and intimidation. Speech which challenges "politically correct" doctrine is often shouted down. Or relegated to tightly-restricted "free speech zones." Or deemed unworthy of respectful consideration—even if presented by someone who grew up under Jim Crow (see, for example, the protests against Condoleezza Rice's invitation to be Rutgers' 2014 commencement speaker).

The point here is that all of us (whether on the Left or the Right) are capable of trampling on the freedoms of others. And the danger appears to be particularly great when one holds considerable power—as the white supremacists did in the Jim Crow South and as progressives do on today's college campuses.

Now, none of this would surprise our nation's founders (who had their own shortcomings, lest we forget). As James Madison famously said, "If men were angels, no government would be necessary." And part of the reason Madison penned the First Amendment is so that the public square could be filled with the vigorous exchange of (both popular and unpopular) ideas.

To be sure, few Americans have ever exercised their free speech rights as effectively as Patricia Stephens and her fellow FAMU students. Which is why all of us should seek to learn from—and follow—these college students' courageous example.

Cancel Culture is All Around Us

American thought leader Scott Adams,' the *Dilbert* creator, satirist, and cartoonist, was interviewed by the *Epoch Times* in 2019 and from that article is some great advice to live by regarding cancel culture:

The "48-hour" rule says that if you've done something dumb–usually you've misspoken, or maybe you said exactly what you meant but it was a bad thing to say–you have 48 hours to clarify and/or apologize. If you hit that, (if) it's a reasonable apology, has to be a pretty good one, or a reasonable clarification, (then) we as a society should say: 48 hours–(he) saw a problem. (He) did what he could do.

Now the other rule is the "20-year" rule. I suggest the "20-year" rule. If something happened more than twenty years ago–unless you're a pedophile, or a murderer or something–that we let it go, because you're just not the same person. It's very close to blaming a different person for your crime because every cell in your body has been replaced. The way you think, the way you act, is almost certainly different over twenty years.

Criticisms of cancel culture centered on the feeling that people were becoming too keen to ruin lives over mistakes made many years ago. That people didn't get a second chance. That social media is too quick to pile on and police increasingly high standards of political correctness and do so in a way that simply is virtue signaling and performatively woke.

That canceling has gone too far and simply become a way of rejecting anyone you disagreed with or someone who did something you didn't like. Former President Barack Obama notably criticized cancel culture (though not using the words as such), arguing that easy social media judgments don't amount to true social activism.

Viewpoint Diversity, Intellectual Humility & Sapience

The Campus Expression Survey (CES) from 1,078 currently enrolled college students in the United States was developed by members of Heterodox Academy in response to students and professors who say they feel like they are "walking on eggshells," not just in the classroom but in informal interactions on campus as well.

This chapter captures their report and presents a summary of all of the CES data Heterodox Academy has obtained to date. These analyses revealed a number of interesting findings, including:

- 53% of students surveyed reported that they do not think their college or university frequently encourages students to consider a wide variety of viewpoints and perspectives.

- 32% of conservatives (vs. 8% of liberals) were very reluctant to discuss politics in the classroom.

- 29% of conservatives (vs. 8% of liberals) were very reluctant to discuss gender in the classroom.

- 30% of conservatives (vs. 15% of liberals) were very reluctant to discuss race in the classroom.

- When discussing potentially controversial topics (politics, race, and gender), the students surveyed were most concerned about criticism from their peers followed by criticism or a lower grade from their professor. They were least concerned about criticism on social media or the potential for a harassment complaint against them.

In the intellectual sphere, as it turns out, ideological intolerance is not the monopoly of any particular party. Rather, what we are seeing is a wider, systemic pattern. Oliver Traldi locates it in belief-intensity or "zealousness"—in which the long-documented polarization of the political climate is bleeding into a polarization of the academic sphere. That polarization is being expressed at different levels of the university, against different groups, in different ways.

Bipartisan Problem, Transpartisan Solutions

The academic freedom crisis is multifaceted, covering multiple dimensions of the intensely complicated social fabric of the modern campus. Dr. Jonathan Haidt has focused particularly on students; others have persuasively argued that administrations are a more potent variable; still others have emphasized the role professors have played in the changing campus climate—or the pernicious influence of outside groups.

If approached in a partisan way, it's easy to cherry-pick individual dimensions of the crisis to support a grievance politics that one's own side is being systematically wronged (or wronged more): the Right will point to patterns of disinvitation and a perceived hostile climate for conservative students and faculty driven by left-leaning activists. The Left will point to patterns of faculty dismissal, as well as the professional and media harassment of professors, especially by the Far Right. The result is a systematic, partisan missing of the forest for the trees.

For a principled commitment to speech rights and intellectual pluralism, all of those levels need to be treated with care, judicious examination of data, and appropriate concern. And concern is appropriate—regardless of one's political or ideological commitments.

Cultivate a Campus Culture That Welcomes Diverse Thought and Open Discussion

Given the importance of intellectual inquiry, of subjecting ideas to rigorous back-and-forth testing, it is critically important for universities to cultivate a campus culture that welcomes diverse thought and open discussion—even, or perhaps especially, on controversial topics. And while removing any and all restrictive speech codes is an important first step towards cultivating such a culture, FIRE's ratings don't tell us everything we might like to know about the intellectual "openness" of any school.

After all, just because a particular university has no speech code restrictions does not necessarily mean that its students will feel free to exercise their First Amendment rights—especially if they sense that viewpoints other than their own are "privileged" on campus. Accordingly, it may be useful to think of campus speech having a "hierarchy of needs" similar in some ways to those Abraham Maslow identified for the individual.

That is, at the most basic "survival" level, students need legal protections that ensure their right to free expression; but building on this, students need an intellectually-rich environment that fosters respect for diverse viewpoints and allows them to engage in spirited intellectual debate without feeling like they must constantly "walk on eggshells."

Sadly, Dr. Jonathan Haidt and the Heterodox Academy reports that a growing number of the college students he encounters say they pointedly avoid engaging in such spirited discourse—and that this self-censorship often begins in high school.

Unfortunately, when they graduate the most effective policymakers that weave together the best ideas from a range of perspectives in order to address society's most intractable problems will be lacking.

The Campus Expression Survey (CES) was developed by members of the Heterodox Academy in response to students and professors who say they feel like they are "walking on eggshells," not just in the classroom but in informal interactions on campus as well.

When College Students Self-Censor, Society Loses

Colleges—the intended training ground for the sort of creative and integrative thinking such problem-solving requires—have become increasingly characterized by orthodoxy in what types of questions can be asked and what sort of comments can be shared in the classroom and around campus.

As a result, many students and even some faculty elect to self-censor. As citizens who are counting on students' future contributions to our shared social and civic endeavors, we all suffer when students elect to sit on the sidelines of their own learning or opt-out of scholarship because they feel they do not "belong" at institutions of higher learning.

Indeed, it is vital for America's future to encourage a diversity of opinions on college campuses. But what will it take to achieve that goal?

Academic stakeholders must create campuses eager to welcome professors, students and speakers who approach problems and questions from different points of view, explicitly valuing the role such diversity plays in advancing the pursuit of knowledge, discovery, and innovation.

Rather than merely tolerating fellow learners whose views are wildly different from one's own, all should seek out and cherish that difference.

Because we see things differently, we will be better able to explore the nuances of the topics we study, deepening our understanding and thus equipping us to be better able to move the needle on those issues we care about most.

This is Not a Left-Right Issue

This is about creating intellectual institutions where learners can come together, humbled by their incomplete knowledge, curious what they can learn from others, able to share their own ideas and perspectives and eager to think together with nuance, open minds, respect and goodwill—all in service to understanding the complexities of our world more deeply.

The concept of constructive disagreement centers around creating a dynamic where key stakeholders in an organization can and are compelled to disagree. The word constructive alludes to the need to raise issues, debate, and resolve them. In the academy, this no longer or rarely happens--but it does in the corporate world.

To achieve that goal in academia where it's sorely lacking, academic stakeholders must enact policies and practices that support heterodox classrooms and campuses. This requires three ingredients:

First, stakeholders must value open inquiry and constructive disagreement. The good news is the available data suggest students, faculty and administrators overwhelmingly do value these things (in principle).

Second, stakeholders must have access to, or be willing to create, effective strategies for enacting these values. For students, this could mean forming or participating in freedom of speech organizations or related initiatives.

For professors, it could be about strategies they deploy in the classroom to create an environment conducive to open inquiry and constructive disagreement or signaling a desire for viewpoint diversity in job ads during faculty searches.

In other cases, it's as simple as the chief academic officer being a vocal and visible cheerleader for the role constructive disagreement across lines of difference plays in realizing the very mission of the institution.

Other interventions are a heavier lift, like actually following through on the consequences stated in an existing policy even when there's tremendous social pressure to do otherwise. Organizations like Heterodox Academy, OpenMind and Village Square continue to design and distribute tools and resources to support these efforts of administrators and faculty.

Third, stakeholders must perceive social permission to act on these values. This is a tougher nut to crack. For instance, even if professors set a good tone, students could be concerned about social sanction from peers.

Many of America's colleges and universities have fallen into a narrow orthodoxy in what is acceptable to say and to think on campus. Now is the time for all of us who value the pursuit of knowledge to support a new heterodoxy that welcomes, supports, and encourages a diversity of viewpoints.

The concept of constructive disagreement centers around creating a dynamic where key stakeholders in the faculty and student body are compelled to disagree. The word constructive alludes to the need to raise issues, debate, and resolve them reasonably. In the academy, this no longer or rarely happens--but it does so in the corporate world.

Our future as the world's leader in higher-education innovation depends on it.

Viewpoint Diversity on Campus is Essential

Viewpoint diversity refers to the state of a community or group in which members approach questions or problems from multiple perspectives. When a community is marked by intellectual humility, empathy, trust, and curiosity, viewpoint diversity gives rise to engaged and civil debate, constructive disagreement, and shared progress towards truth. Viewpoint diversity enables colleges and universities to realize their twin goals of producing the best research and providing the best education.

As citizens who are counting on students' and researchers' future contributions to our shared social, civic, moral, and scientific endeavors, we all suffer when orthodoxies distort and limit understanding of the social, aesthetic, and natural world—or when institutions of higher learning are unable to draw in perspectives from the whole of society. To help solve this problem we need heterodox academies.

To make headway on solving the world's most complex problems, scholars and policy makers must deploy the best ideas. This typically requires consulting a wide range of perspectives.

While a community of inquiry defined by intellectual humility, curiosity, empathy, and trust may hold many beliefs in common, few ideas will be beyond discussion, revision, or good-faith debate.

The Surest Sign of an Unhealthy Scholarly Culture is the Presence of Orthodoxy

Orthodoxies are most readily apparent when people fear shame, ostracism, or any other form of social or professional retaliation for questioning or challenging a commonly held idea.

The best way to defend against orthodoxies—or to neutralize them—is to foster commitment to open inquiry, viewpoint diversity and constructive disagreement. When these elements are missing, orthodoxies can take root and thrive.

Viewpoint diversity occurs when members of a group or community approach problems or questions from a range of perspectives. Institutions of higher learning face several interrelated viewpoint diversity deficits including:

- Racial/Ethnic
- Socioeconomic
- Geographical
- Religious
- Political
- And in many fields, Gender

Academic freedom demanded a respect for a diversity of views. During the Vietnam War years, college campuses were alive with debates about the war and a host of other subjects. There was no effort to silence diverse points of view.

Per Dr. Jonathan Haidt, the future of liberal democracy depends in no small measure on empathy—the ability to humanize and understand others and tolerance. Students need to see those with whom they disagree politically as people—or else they risk alienating and demonizing the other side, which only leads to further conflict and highly-limited understanding.

A culture that will not tolerate divergence of opinion harms students, but academic research is also at risk when dominant theories and opinions no longer encounter counterclaims that test their validity.

Viewpoint Diversity Deficits Can Lead to Intolerance

When environments lack sufficient viewpoint diversity, problematic assumptions can go unchallenged, promising ideas and methods can go underexplored, and it can be difficult to effectively understand or engage with others who have different backgrounds, priors, and commitments.

For instance, to the extent that institutions of higher learning lack viewpoint diversity (and are thus not representative of the broader societies in which they are embedded), scholars may struggle to communicate the value and relevance of their work to people outside the academy in an accessible and compelling way.

Well-intentioned social programs can fail in their stated aims—or even cause harm—when the people designing policies are too far removed from the populations their interventions are intended to serve. Meanwhile, young people from underrepresented groups may come to feel as though they don't belong in the academy—and decline to apply to college, drop out midway through, or pursue non-academic paths if they push through to graduation.

In short, we would have reasons to recruit and retain a more diverse pool of faculty, staff, and students even if the lack of viewpoint diversity were purely the result of differences in interests and priorities among members of various groups.

However, we know that many disparities are also—at least in part—the result of a hostile atmosphere, discrimination, a lack of access or institutional dynamics that tend to privilege certain groups for reasons other than the quality of their research or ideas. It seems important to rectify these imbalances for moral as well as practical reasons.

Restoring Free Speech on Campus

Restrictions on free expression on college campuses are incompatible with the fundamental values of higher education. At public institutions, they violate the First Amendment; at most private institutions, they break faith with stated commitments to academic freedom. And these restrictions are widespread.

The good news is that the types of restrictions discussed in this section can be reformed. A student or faculty member can be a tremendously effective advocate for change when he or she is aware of expressive rights and is willing to engage administrators in defense of them. Public exposure is also critical to defeating speech codes since universities are often unwilling to defend their speech codes in the face of public criticism.

Unconstitutional policies also can be defeated in court, especially at public universities, where speech codes have been struck down in federal courts across the country. Many more such policies have been revised in favor of free speech as the result of legal settlements.

Any speech code in force at a public university is vulnerable to a constitutional challenge. Moreover, as speech codes are consistently defeated in court, administrators cannot credibly argue that they are unaware of the law, which means that they may be held personally liable when they are responsible for their schools' violations of constitutional rights.

Censorship in the academic community is commonplace. Students and faculty are increasingly being investigated and punished for controversial, dissenting or simply discomforting speech. It's time for colleges and universities to take a deep breath, remember who they are and reaffirm their fundamental commitment to freedom of expression.

The suppression of free speech at institutions of higher education is a matter of great national concern. However, by working together with universities to revise restrictive speech codes and to reaffirm commitments to free expression, we can continue to stride toward campuses that truly embody the "marketplace of ideas" that such institutions must be in our society.

With these issues and goals in mind, in 2015, the University of Chicago convened a Committee on Freedom of Expression to do exactly that. The committee issued a statement identifying the principles that must guide institutions committed to attaining knowledge through free and open discourse. Guaranteeing members of the academic community "the broadest possible latitude to speak, write, listen, challenge, and learn," the statement guarantees students and faculty the right "to discuss any problem that presents itself."

The Chicago Statement (Committee on Freedom of Expression)

How should students and scholars respond when challenged by speech with which they disagree, or that they even loathe? The Chicago Statement (Committee on Freedom of Expression) sets forth the answer: "by openly and vigorously contesting the ideas that they oppose." Anticipating the push and pull of passionate debate, the statement sets forth important ground rules: "Debate or deliberation may not be suppressed because the ideas put forth are thought by some or even by most members of the University community to be offensive, unwise, immoral, or wrong-headed."

Perhaps most important, the Chicago statement makes clear that "it is not the proper role of the University to attempt to shield individuals from ideas and opinions they find unwelcome, disagreeable, or even deeply offensive." Laura Kipnis, Alice Dreger, and Teresa Buchanan would have benefited from this frank and necessary recognition.

"Because the University is committed to free and open inquiry in all matters, it guarantees all members of the University community the broadest possible latitude to speak, write, listen, challenge, and learn."– The Chicago Statement.

Since last year's report, FIRE has observed an increase in the adoption of free speech statements at colleges and universities inspired by the "Report of the Committee on Freedom of Expression" at the University of Chicago (better known as the "Chicago Statement"). As of May 2019, 63 institutions or faculty bodies have adopted or endorsed the Chicago Principles or a substantially similar policy statement.

Thousands more need to follow!

Adopting the Chicago Statement

All colleges that are seriously committed to free inquiry and robust debate should consider adopting a version of the Chicago Statement. In doing so, the college not only reaffirms its core purpose as a place for discourse and debate, but also encourages the campus community to engage in such expression. By actively prioritizing free speech in this manner, universities can outline a set of principles that will become the hallmark of the community they aspire to build.

As eloquently described in the Chicago Statement, "fostering the ability of members of the University community to engage in such debate and deliberation in an effective and responsible manner is an essential part of the University's educational mission." That is the type of campus community FIRE and HxA hope all colleges will aim to cultivate.

When institutional leaders wait until controversy erupts on campus to publicly endorse free speech, detractors often accuse well-meaning administrators of favoring one side over the other. A proactive endorsement of free expression principles effectively shuts down any criticism that the university is picking sides in the latest campus controversy. Why wait until a controversial speaker comes to campus or racist posters fill your residence halls to take a principled stand on free speech? Instead, consider adopting a free expression statement today.

The Chicago Statement Can Take Three Different Forms

As tracked by FIRE, endorsement of the Chicago Statement may take three different forms: official adoption by a university, approval by a governing board, or endorsement by a faculty body. Additionally, to ensure campus-wide engagement with the free speech issues raised by the Chicago Statement, many institutions choose to include several other stakeholders in the process, such as the student government and other campus community members.

Backed by a strong commitment to freedom of expression and academic freedom, faculty could challenge one another, their students, and the public to consider new possibilities, without fear of reprisal. Students would no longer face punishment for exercising their right to speak out freely about the issues most important to them.

Instead of learning that voicing one's opinions invites silencing, students would be taught that spirited debate is a vital necessity for the advancement of knowledge. And they would be taught that the proper response to ideas they oppose is not censorship, but argument on the merits. That, after all, is what a university is for.

6 – Academy at the Crossroads and Campus Perils to Western Civilization

From the Jacob Howland "The Campus Peril to Western Civilization" *City Journal* October 2023 article:

Informed observers have known for some time that our universities are broken. But the cheerleading on American campuses for terrorists who unleashed a pogrom of a magnitude and viciousness not seen since the Holocaust has made it clear that the collapse of higher education imperils Western civilization itself. Without real higher education, we would forget the past and stumble blindly into the future. Without universities worthy of the name, there would be no civilization.

Higher education exists to preserve, transmit, and extend knowledge, including the sound judgment and knowledge of the whole we call wisdom. Universities stand at the threshold between past and future, self and society, the eternal verities above and the flow of time below. Their job is to join what would otherwise fall apart: to remember the past, fructify the present, and incubate the future. At their best, they are modern temples of Janus, the two-faced Roman god who looks backward and forward, inward and outward—a symbol of wakeful, vigilant minds that receive tradition with gratitude, seek knowledge with grace, and face challenges with grit.

81

But in the United States, universities have never been worse than they are today. Barbarians have invaded the temples of teaching and learning, ransacked the sanctuaries, and defiled the sacred scrolls. For decades, students have been steeped in a postmodern intellectual culture of repudiation, relativism, and reductivism.

They've been taught to "deconstruct" the great books and noble ideals of the West; to regard morality, and even the criteria of scientific truth, as social constructions; and to understand politics and society as "discourses of power" illuminated by the doctrines of "critical theory" and "intersectionality." Bereft of precious civilizational compasses and maps, they have learned to regard fundamental social relationships as zero-sum games of domination and servitude.

The Campus Perils to Western Civilization

The events of recent weeks have brought home an ugly truth: far from equipping students to preserve and extend civilization, American universities—especially elite ones—have been teaching them how to destroy it. They've reminded a forgetful public that pernicious academic theories can have appalling consequences.

As private equity investor and Penn alumnus Marc Rowan wrote in a letter to the University of Pennsylvania condemning the institution's platforming of anti-Semitism on campus, "words and ideas matter." The way that students, professors, and academic administrators have welcomed the real-world application of hateful ideas leaves no doubt on this point.

At Georgetown, Students for Justice in Palestine posted signs explaining that "decolonization" is not just "an abstract academic theory" but a "tangible event." Hamas's efforts at tangible decolonization included burning families alive. Pathologists at Israel's National Center of Forensic Medicine have been working hard to identify 297 bodies so brutalized as to be unrecognizable.

An article reports that Chen Kugel, the Center's director, "wept as he described how they had received remains so disfigured they had to perform a CT scan to understand there were two bodies. One big, one small." "You can tell from the shapes of their spines that it is an adult and a child, and they are sitting together and they are hugging tightly together," he said. "In their final moments. They were burnt to death like this. Cremated alive in their own home, clutching one another."

It's bad enough that university students have enthusiastically supported such horrific acts. But it's not as though they leave behind their schooling in postmodern doctrines and revolutionary ideologies when they graduate. Many go on to assume influential positions in education, media, culture, and politics, where they proceed to indoctrinate others. Elite universities are primary feeders in all these areas, especially higher education. A 2012 study, for example, found that "the top 11 institutions were responsible for half the faculty doctorates" in political science. The same is probably true of most academic fields.

Some radicalized graduates now teach at elite universities, like the Cornell professor who told a rally in support of Hamas that those who "weren't exhilarated" by Hamas's actions "would not be human," or the one at the University of Michigan who tore down posters of kidnapped Israelis.

Some become journalists at major newspapers like the New York Times and the *Washington Post*, both of which immediately reported that Israel was responsible for a missile attack that struck a hospital in Gaza, killing 500 people—except that the missile didn't hit the hospital (it landed in the parking lot), didn't kill 500 people, and apparently wasn't launched by Israel.

Others become directors and curators at major art museums, where they cultivate racial resentment and anti-Western attitudes by lecturing visitors about white supremacy and colonialism. Still others enter government, where genuinely totalitarian ideas—like Hillary Clinton's suggestion that Trump supporters should be "formally deprogrammed"—are now aired openly. (In practice, that would require the kind of reeducation camps China has established for the Uyghurs.)

The saddest thing about the collapse of higher education may not be that it bodes so ill for our country's future, though that is certainly depressing. It is that our nation's most esteemed universities, and many others to boot, have defrauded their students. They've cheated them of a once-in-a-lifetime opportunity to receive a real education: one that opens their minds to the deep pleasures of learning, and to the precious inheritance of knowledge and wisdom that has sustained civilization for millennia.

So what is to be done? There are two ways forward: attempt to reform existing institutions, and found new ones. Both paths are worth trying.

First, alumni must speak up, and, if necessary, close their checkbooks.

The short letter to Penn president Liz Magill written by Jon Huntsman, former U.S. ambassador and governor of Utah, shows how it's done. Universities depend on the generosity of graduates who are grateful for their education and have fond memories of their time on campus. But those warm feelings should not blind them to what is happening at their alma maters. I graduated from Swarthmore College, where Students for Justice in Palestine praised Hamas "martyrs" for resisting the "imperialist apparatus" of Zionism. President Valerie Smith responded with unconscionable equivocation. I've contributed thousands of dollars to Swarthmore over the past three decades, but when Smith ignored my email, I told her Never Again. Imagine if thousands of alumni did the same.

Still, it's unlikely that elite institutions will change course. The moral and intellectual rot has gone too far. Donors should find more deserving institutions to support and should place strict conditions on their gifts. Universities must dismantle their diversity, equity, and inclusion offices and eliminate oaths in hiring and tenure to support DEI imperatives. As Peter Berkowitz has written, the "fine words" of DEI "conceal the divisive ambition to vilify the supposed oppressors and exalt the supposed oppressed." (That ambition was openly expressed after the Hamas attacks by a DEI director at Cornell, not in fine words but in expletives.)

Every college and university in America claims to support academic freedom and open discourse. These words, too, are honored more in the breach than the observance. Donors and alumni should demand that institutions live up to them. They should support initiatives that cultivate the virtues of reflective openness and civility, including the new schools of civic leadership that have been founded, or are under construction, at Arizona State, the University of Texas, and the University of North Carolina, among others. And they should push to rebuild genuinely liberal education, which has been progressively dismantled at many institutions since Jesse Jackson led chants of "Hey, hey, ho, ho, Western Civ has got to go" at Stanford in 1987.

The other way forward is to found new universities.

That's an expensive and complicated undertaking, but it makes it possible to begin with a clean slate. UATX offers a model of such educational entrepreneurship, one that emphasizes the public as well as personal blessings of a liberal education.

UATX champions academic freedom—"the right to think the unthinkable, discuss the unmentionable, and challenge the unchallengeable"—not for its own sake, but as a means to discover truth. Human flourishing, and its civilizational preconditions, are central to our curriculum. We require all students to study the Hebrew and Christian scriptures, the Greek poets and philosophers, and Confucius; to learn about Islam and European identity; to reflect on the nature of modernity and the uses and abuses of technology; to study the American experiment in liberty and the ideological tyrannies of the twentieth century; and to acquire the basic scientific, technical, economic, and entrepreneurial knowledge they will need to succeed in the twenty-first century.

Human beings desire not just to know, but to put their knowledge into practice. All UATX students must undertake a substantial project to discover or build something that serves the human good. These undertakings will help them to discover how their greatest passions might meet humanity's greatest needs. Along the way, they will develop essential skills and virtues of cooperation, communication, resilience, imagination, and flexibility.

The philosopher Eugen Rosenstock-Huessy defined the citizen as "a person who, if need be, can re-found his civilization." Civilization is collapsing today, and such individuals are needed more than ever before. Whatever form new institutions and programs may take, they must above all aim to educate citizens.

Jacob Howland is Provost and Dean of Intellectual Foundations at UATX. His latest book is *Glaucon's Fate: History, Myth, and Character in Plato's Republic*.

The Academy at the Crossroads and it's War on the West

Per the Heather Mac Donald "The Academy at the Crossroads, Part Two: Penn 2.0 and the larger ideological problem: universities are waging a war on the West" *City Journal* December 2023 report:

The pro-Hamas uprising that broke out across American universities after October 7, 2023, roused once-somnolent alumni and donors. That awakening has now produced a new university charter, called a "Vision for a New Future of the University of Pennsylvania," drafted by Penn professors. Penn's most recent president, Liz Magill, had to resign on December 9, 2023, following widely mocked testimony at a congressional hearing on campus anti-Semitism.

The charter's authors, along with Penn's rebel donors, hope to make agreement with the new constitution a requirement for Penn's new president. If enough Penn constituents, especially faculty, endorse it, the board of trustees will be compelled to adopt such a prerequisite, their thinking goes. An ongoing donation boycott provides the financial pressure. Ultimately, alumni across the country may be inspired to seek a similar foundational shake-up in their own alma maters, the drafters hope.

The new constitution adopts the thinking behind the Kalven Report, drafted in 1967 at the University of Chicago. Penn must henceforth abstain from adopting an institutional position on political issues. Embracing an official line alienates dissenting members of the university who might want to challenge "common orthodoxies," explains the charter. Individual members of the university, by contrast, shall be free to propose, test, and reject the "widest spectrum of perspectives."

The university's selection committees have one mission only: identifying excellence. Hiring non-excellent diversity candidates makes it harder to attract outstanding faculty and students. (This assertion will seem commonsensical to anyone who believes in merit. The diversity complex would respond that, to the contrary, faculty and students shun non-"diverse" institutions. Sadly, in some cases, especially in the case of woke students, the diversity complex is correct. That does not make Penn 2.0 wrong, however, to seek to break the stranglehold of diversity thinking.) The new constitution posits that an unambiguous, publicly understood commitment to excellence will give Penn a competitive edge in hiring and student admissions in the decades ahead. This, too, seems commonsensical. Testing such a hypothesis is long overdue.

Penn 2.0 overcomes in one stroke a weakness bedeviling a central strategy of campus reform.

Those seeking to create new universities face the challenge that no new institution can offer the prize that a legacy university confers: status and bragging rights. It is prestige that drives the ever-more frenzied torrent of college applications, rather than any promise of knowledge. The beauty of the Penn 2.0 plan is that it re-founds Penn on a new footing, while maintaining Penn's prestige-granting power.

Were Penn 2.0 to become part of the presidential hiring search, it would be clarifying to see how many university apparatchiks demurred from its principles. Penn's temporary replacement for ousted president Magill shows how heavy a lift Penn 2.0 is going to be. Penn's trustees chose J. Larry Jameson, now dean of Penn's medical school, to serve as the university's interim president.

As soon as Jameson took over the medical school in 2011, he placed diversity hiring and indoctrination at the core of his administration. He created the school's first vice dean for Inclusion and Diversity and first associate dean for Diversity and Inclusion. Naturally, an Office of Inclusion and Diversity followed, which rolled out endless diversity initiatives and mandates, including Health Equity Weeks, the Transgender Patient Advocate program, and the LGBT Student-Trainee-Faculty Mentorship program.

In 2021, Jameson initiated what the Penn press office called a "new institution-wide program aimed at eliminating structural racism." (Hint: There is no structural racism at the Penn medical school. The medical school, like the rest of the university, is desperate to admit and hire as many blacks and Hispanics as possible, often disregarding academic skills gaps to do so.)

As with all such duplicative programs, the conceit of the 2021 "institution-wide" antiracism initiative was that the school was for the first time prioritizing "diversity" at "all levels of staffing."

Jameson, in other words, would scorn the proposed new constitution if asked to stay in the presidential post permanently. And the trustees who put him in the interim position presumably support his diversity crusade, since it has been impossible to miss during his med-school tenure.

Do the rebel donors have the financial clout to force the charter on the university anyway? They are bargaining on the fact that the Wharton School of Business, from which many of the close-the-checkbook participants graduated, contributes the lion's share of philanthropic support to the university at large, according to their analysis.

If Wharton feels seriously squeezed, the effect would cascade more widely.

The gargantuan size of university endowments, including Penn's $21 billion, might seem to make higher education boycott-proof. But universities, though viewing themselves as unsullied by the pollution of money-grubbing, inequity-producing capitalism, are greedy bastards. They feel entitled to every last (private-sector-generated) penny that may be coming their way. Any drop-off in donations causes them teeth-gnashing agony.

It remains to be seen how much financial pain the alumni dissenters can inflict and what its effect will be.

For every alumnus who now perceives his university's intellectual betrayals, many others undoubtedly back the aims of the intersectional university. This ratio will only grow with every new generation of graduates.

Any university reform movement is running a race against time.

It is not hard to imagine a counter-fundraising push from those alumni who agree with the antiracism agenda. The head of the Penn alumni association early on expressed the association's support for the now-departed university president and chairman of the board. While the financial battle takes shape, however, the donor rebellion needs to sharpen its positions to ensure its greatest chance of success.

First of all, the donors need to clean up their stance on free speech.

They have heretofore faced two options.

- They could take the high road and demand free speech across the board: for opponents of preferences, say, and for opponents of Israel.
- Or they could adopt in reverse the same double standards that have been so nauseatingly on display in every pronouncement about a university's undying commitment to academic freedom.

Too many alumni have taken the second course.

While rebuking their school's intellectual monoculture and intolerance of dissent, they demand the silencing of anti-Zionist speech in the same breath. They may do so in the name of playing the college's own double standards against it, but the result is to legitimate those double standards all the same.

They have adopted the same distinctions utilized by the campus Left: "hate speech" is not "free speech," and deserves no protections. They want college presidents to exercise a preclearance function over anti-Israel speakers and conferences, such as Penn's controversial Palestine Writes Literature Festival. Some seek to outlaw the Boycott, Divest, and Sanction movement. Some seek to enshrine the wildly overbroad definition of anti-Semitism from the International Holocaust Remembrance Alliance.

But however odious the student chants of "intifada, intifada" and "glory to our martyrs," however shocking professorial tweets calling Hamas's attacks "exhilarating" and "extraordinary," such speech should be punished only if it directly incites violence, or if the speaker physically harasses or threatens someone.

Banning such utterances will not erase the beliefs behind them; it is better to have those beliefs out in the open, where they can be challenged and their sources identified.

Second, the donors must avoid the rhetoric of safetyism.

Calling for the protection of "unsafe" Jewish students, when that unsafety is primarily a psychological state, will only strengthen the therapeutic academy, to the long-term detriment of free thought. Jewish students understandably feel under siege when their classmates cheer on Hamas, but such expression is protected under free-speech principles.

While physical attack or incitement to imminent violence must be criminally prosecuted, and its perpetrators expelled, there have thankfully been few such incidents. Indeed, a Harvard student organizing Jewish alumni against the school admitted to me that he feels under no physical threat walking on campus. A Jewish Princeton student said the same.

As of December 14, 2023, no violence or physical confrontations had taken place at Yale involving Jewish students. Yes, some Jewish students are in fear for their lives on their campuses, but civil order will need to break down much further for that to be a realistic assessment.

Donors and alumni should remember that it was in the name of fighting "hate" and protecting student "safety" that the campus diversity bureaucracy reached its present proportions and power. Absent a transformation in campus personnel, bolstering the authority to quell alleged hate and safeguard intellectual and psychological "safety" will be used overwhelmingly against views and speakers deemed conservative.

Alumni might also want to tone down their own rhetoric regarding campus anti-Semitism just a bit. Rowan suggested that Penn's hosting of the Palestine Writes Literature Festival legitimated the "horrific attacks in Israel." David Magerman, a former overseer of the Penn engineering school, wrote then-president Magill on October 15, 2023, criticizing what he called her "fierce support for the Hamas-affiliated speakers at the Palestine Writes festival."

Magill had never supported the "Hamas-affiliated speakers," however, only the (belatedly discovered) principle of free speech. Magerman accused her of being "ambivalent to the unprecedented evil" that Hamas's terror attacks on Israel represented. By the end of his letter, Magill had gone from being ambivalent about evil to supporting it, and the speakers at the festival had gone from being "affiliated" with Hamas—even that a stretch—to being Hamas members themselves.

By virtue of "hosting Hamas on campus, and . . . failing to call Hamas evil," Penn "supports evil," in Magerman's analysis. Such language is undoubtedly heartfelt, but it risks painting its users, in the eyes of the opposition, as blinded by emotion.

The biggest course correction is to broaden the diagnosis of the university's current pathology.

By psychologizing the pathology as one of anti-Semitism, and by demanding that the university fight this psychological problem, the alumni are walking into a trap. Asking college bureaucrats to protect Jewish students from anti-Semitism is like threatening to throw Br'er Rabbit into the briar patch. The bureaucrats are only too happy to comply. They have been busily adding new modules on anti-Semitism to existing diversity, equity, and inclusion trainings, all in the name of fighting hate.

Of course, they immediately add that they must also fight Islamophobia, so the diversocrats get a twofer increase to their administrative remit. Rebellious donors may be placated by seeing their campus's sudden commitment to anti-Semitism task forces and diversity trainings and conclude that the crisis is on the way to being solved. But the problem is much deeper than anti-Semitism. And the college administrators are outfoxing the rebel alumni by adopting the rebels' definition of the issue.

The problem is an entire anti-Western ethos that now dominates most of the humanities and social sciences and that in STEM is corroding excellence and meritocracy.

Jews are today seen as the embodiment of that reviled Western civilization, rather than, as in the past, a threat to it. What is today labelled anti-Semitism on college campuses has no connection to the genteel anti-Semitism of the early twentieth century. And yet, college presidents are insisting on just such a lineage.

On October 27, 2023, Harvard president Claudine Gay addressed a Shabbat dinner organized by Harvard's Hillel chapter. She drew a continuous line between Harvard's previous treatment of Jews and what is visible on Harvard Yard today. "Antisemitism has a very long and shameful history at Harvard," she said. "For years, this University has done too little to confront its continuing presence. No longer."

This statement is entirely wrong.

In the 1920s and 1930s, Harvard's WASPs established admissions ceilings to prevent Harvard from becoming Judaicized by Semitic outsiders. But the barriers eventually fell, and Jews became a dominant presence on campus, thanks to their intellectual accomplishments. No one at Harvard today advocates excluding Jews because they don't fit into Harvard's cozy Protestant brotherhood. To the extent that Jews are excluded, it is to make room for academically noncompetitive black and Hispanic students. Such displacement is occurring, but it is not the result of anti-Jewish animus per se.

The majority of today's anti-Semitism comes from a different source than the one Gay alluded to. That source is the intersectional Left, composed of self-proclaimed marginalized groups pretending to be oppressed by phantom white supremacy.

The intersectional Left hates the West, and it hates Jews because they represent the West.

If the essence of the West is what is called in ethnic and postcolonial studies departments "settler colonialism"—which effaces virtuous, ecologically sensitive native peoples of color—then Israel exemplifies a settler colonialist, genocidal state.

91

To test Gay's assertion of an unbroken connection between Harvard's past and present anti-Semitism, imagine that Harvard still discriminates against Jews because they are not clubbable, yet Harvard has no academic departments promoting the idea that the West is responsible for the world's injustices, and no diversity bureaucracy telling students of color that they are victims of Harvard's racism.

Would students still be screaming "From the River to the Sea, Palestine Will be Free!" and "Long Live Our Martyrs?" They would not. Conversely, if Harvard had no history of genteel WASP anti-Semitism but had its present full complement of anti-Western courses, faculty, and fellow-travelling administrators, students would still be channeling Hamas in their banners and chants.

The closest thing on campuses today to traditional anti-Semitism comes from Muslim students and faculty, many of whom have imbibed classic anti-Jewish topoi from birth.

They are joined by "allies" innocent of such propaganda but well-versed in every left-wing indictment against their own civilization. (Those Muslim carriers of the traditional anti-Semitism virus are out of sight in the current discussion of campus anti-Semitism, lest anyone face charges of Islamophobia or a Trumpian lack of appreciation for immigrants. Officially invisible, too, are black anti-Semites, whose century-long strain of anti-Semitism has been unbroken.)

By asserting a genealogy linking historic mainstream anti-Semitism to contemporary academic anti-Semitism, Gay subtly reinforces the unspoken assumption that conservative whites pose the main threat to American Jews—traditionally an article of faith among mainstream Jewish advocacy groups such as the Anti-Defamation League and among liberal Jews themselves.

At the same time, Gay diverts attention from the actual sources of anti-Jewish agitation: the faculty, the curriculum, and Muslims.

The dissident donors need to home in on those sources.

To take just one example: In 2015, Yale president Peter Salovey promised to pour even more funding into Yale's Ethnicity, Race, and Migration (ERM) program. This largesse was part of Salovey's personal crusade against Yale's alleged racism.

The ERM program is emblematic of every such "ethnic" and "postcolonial studies" program across the U.S. According to its course-catalogue description, it "draws from the long-standing fields of U.S. ethnic and Native studies, postcolonial, and subaltern studies but also represents emergent areas like queer of color critique, comparative diaspora studies, critical Muslim and critical refugee studies, race and media studies, feminist science studies, and the environmental humanities." Adumbrated in that roll call are the student coalitions "from the Rockies to the Smokies," to adopt a phrase, that celebrated the Hamas attacks.

Like every ethnic studies program, Yale's ERM concentration unabashedly declares its political nature: "We actively support public-facing and socially engaged scholarship and cultural work," an activist mission that the pro-Hamas demonstrators saw themselves as furthering.

As a lecturer at Harvard's Graduate School of Education told the *Harvard Crimson* earlier this year: "If it is not focused on the project of decolonization, if it is not rooted directly in communities, if it is not intersectional," then it's not Ethnic Studies. And if it is focused on the project of decolonization as an active "community" participant, it belongs nowhere within a university.

Yale professor Zareena Grewal, a documentary filmmaker who teaches in the ERM program, is an embodiment of the ethnic- and post-colonial studies establishment. Grewal's second film for television, Swahili Fighting Words, "traces the legacies of slavery, colonialism, and diasporic identity politics" through Tanzanian rap music. Predictably, she defended the October 7, 2023, attacks since, as she put it, "settlers are not civilians. This is not hard." She added: "My heart is in my throat. Prayers for Palestinians. Israel is a murderous, genocidal settler state and Palestinians have every right to resist through armed struggle, solidarity #FreePalestine."

Such rhetoric is everywhere.

Penn English professor Ania Loomba is another quintessence of the pro-Hamas campus left. Loomba teaches histories of race and colonialism, postcolonial studies, and feminist theory. Her 2021 English class "Can the Subaltern Speak? Identity, Politics and Life-Writing," assigned such pro-revolutionary writers as Antonio Gramsci, Frantz Fanon, and Paulo Freire. Other readings attacked mass incarceration and "race and class in the age of Trump"—because, you know, this was an English class.

Loomba chairs doctoral dissertations on such topics as "The Nation and its Deviants: Global Sexology and the Racial Grammar of Sex in Colonial India, 1870-1950," thus ensuring an unbroken line of identity-based, victim-celebrating academics and a steady stream of students proclaiming their own victimhood or, as a second best alternative, solidarity with local nonwhite victims.

Some donors have convinced themselves that the problem with universities lies with the students and with the admission process, rather than with the faculty, curriculum, and administrators. A nascent Jewish alumni group at MIT will demand that the school screen out anti-Semites—something that would embroil a school in a host of legal complications, if it were even possible.

But though a few freshmen may arrive at first-year orientation already able to ape the formulae of ethnic and postcolonial studies, most of them pick up those verbal gestures and concomitant political attitudes from their courses and from legacy campus political groups.

The exquisitely grandiose rhetoric in a Cornell University student manifesto drafted after the Hamas attacks was learned on-site: "We begin fully cognizant that power concedes nothing without demand, and thus we refuse any longer to beg this institution for concessions—instead, we issue undeniable ultimatums," began Cornell's Coalition for Mutual Liberation on November 9, 2023, recalling the Black Panther Party's shaky command of the English idiom.

The Coalition for Mutual Liberation and its ally, Black Students United, were "united in solidarity for Palestine in order to reject imperialism and white supremacy everywhere," they wrote. "We believe that the Palestinian struggle is part of intersecting efforts to achieve the complete liberation of all colonized and oppressed peoples." Leave the academic roots of such student posturing unchallenged, and nothing will change.

There is one benefit to keeping the alumni revolt focused on eradicating alleged campus anti-Semitism, however. Any university's gestures toward doing so will crack the intersectional university apart. What the university mainstream, such as it is, is now calling "anti-Semitism" is for the university Left expressions of simple fact.

What, then, will the forthcoming sensitivity training modules on "anti-Semitism" look like? No more "River to Sea" chants? No more accusations of settler colonialism? No more divestment calls (even if such calls are not banned)? How will the DEI trainers take up their new task since many of them are part of the anti-Zionist coalition?

For now, the campus Left is sitting on its hands and staying silent as its core beliefs are reviled by campus administrators and by the Democratic Party establishment. But it is hard to imagine such self-discipline lasting. And when that self-control finally breaks down, the results will be enthralling to watch.

Focus on alleged campus anti-Semitism has been a valuable organizing tool.

The charge of anti-Semitism caught the attention above all of the Jewish donors whose support over the decades has been central to the ballooning of university endowments. Those few faculty members who have steadfastly opposed the politicization of the university are less than impressed by their newfound allies.

A Penn professor told me: The "handful of outraged trustees [and donors] should have understood everything dumb, dysfunctional, politicized, and discriminatory at Penn thirty years ago. They lavished love, approval, and mountains of money on the administration. Nowhere have trustees honored their primary fiduciary obligation to pass on a free, fair, and rigorous university to posterity."

This professor, Jewish himself, concludes: "If I had to bet, the liberal Jews will be lured back into the fold, since they object only to anti-Semitism and they love the prestige of having buildings named after them."

There are signs that this pessimistic prediction may not be borne out, even if GOP politicians intend to keep their focus on easily graspable anti-Semitism. In a December 12 letter to Penn's board of trustees, Rowan wrote that anti-Semitism "is just a symptom of a larger problem: culture."

His definition of that culture is vague (or euphemistic): it has "allowed for preferred versus free speech" and has distracted from the university's core mission of excellence. Rowan is being too accommodationist. The larger problem is ideological. Universities are waging a war on the West. Israel is just its current manifestation.

Any optimism about the current moment must be tempered. There have been other efforts, most notably by journalist and activist David Horowitz, to make universities honor their obligation to pass on a civilizational inheritance with love and gratitude. They all failed. But this time feels different.

The sheer scope of attention that has been focused on the university, the array of powerful individuals who are mobilized, the daily revelations about conflicts of interest and shameless double standards, provide momentum that, if maintained, could result in actual change.

To be sure, the beneficiaries and perpetrators of the intersectional status quo outnumber the rebels; they make up the vast majority of the administration, the majority of professors and vast majority of graduate students in non-STEM fields, and a growing number of faculty and administrators even in STEM.

Trustees are either deliberately oblivious to this reality or agents of it. Nevertheless, as one rebel donor told me, all it takes on corporate boards sometimes is one or two determined trustees to turn around a company.

With the Penn 2.0 charter as a template and with enough persistence on the part of the rebels, the next generation of college students may have real opportunities, beyond today's handful of contrarian colleges, to immerse themselves in beauty, sublimity, and the wonder of knowledge.

7 – Alumni, Trustees & School Boards Push Back Against DEI Indoctrination

Credit: KATV.

Per the Jay Schalin "Bolstering the Board: Trustees Are Academia's Best Hope for Reform" The James G. Martin Center for Academic Renewal report in July 2020:

Higher education is approaching an existential crisis. It is in danger of rejecting its most fundamental value, the search for truth, and replacing it with political dogma and opportunistic careerism. Other problems abound, but none so serious as this one.

Indeed, in many departments on many campuses—even on campuses that seem well-ordered—the spirit of free inquiry is under attack. Irrational theories, such as the belief that race and gender are mere social constructs, are proliferating. Political correctness and corporate and government money are distorting scientific exploration. Many departments are dominated by adherents of fundamentally flawed philosophies, such as French post-modernism or communism.

Bolstering the Board: Trustees Are Academia's Best Hope for Reform

Disturbed or hostile individuals are routinely hired, while conservative scholars "need not apply" to many departments. On occasion, even political liberals who express moderate views in public are hounded out of their jobs; one widely publicized incident occurred in 2018 at Evergreen State University when a liberal biology professor, Bret Weinstein, was forced to resign because of harassment from students after he refused to leave campus on a specified "day of absence" for white people.

Certainly, much of academia is still functioning at high levels, in technological research and STEM (science, technology, engineering, and mathematics) education, for instance. But the continued success of some programs merely provides cover for the erosion of standards and quality elsewhere in the Ivory Tower.

In much of the humanities and social sciences, political dogma has already replaced objective inquiry. In some schools of education, for example, science is considered dependent upon the background of the individual instead of having universal principles for all, with indigenous myths considered equal to rigorous research methods.

It is still possible to get an excellent education at many universities, even in the humanities. But it is not likely to happen by chance; either a student must be intensely focused on a career path in the financial or empirical fields, or he or she will need considerable guidance and awareness to make it through the maze of nonsense. And the maze is getting increasingly difficult to maneuver.

How can this be happening in plain sight, without spurring a massive campaign for reform?

In a well-run higher education system based on the honest pursuit of truth, the marketplace of ideas would permit critics to attack, refute, and even satirize such ideas. The worst theories would be prevented from gaining even a tiny foothold; the rest would be condemned to some musty little corner while more reasoned ideas displaced them. But that is not the case; the free market of ideas is broken, replaced by a one-sided, dogmatic consensus.

At the heart of the problem is higher education's tradition of sharing governance functions and authority among the board, the administration, and the faculty. Few observers are willing to criticize it; it is truly a "sacred cow."

The prescriptions of experts for fixing higher education's problems call for more of the same practices that led to the crisis in the first place. That is, most of the acclaimed writers call for heightening the shared components of higher education governance, not reducing them.

But that may be the worst thing institutions can do. If higher education's governance practices are working, why then is academia increasingly struggling to protect its most important goals? To increase the shared component of governance by empowering faculty and administrators is to essentially do more of the same thing that causes the current failure to correct the problems.

For shared governance, by definition, inhibits reform

It is based on developing a consensus among widely differing constituencies, and therefore tends to clog and tangle rather than attack problems directly. If you wish to maintain the status quo, instituting a system with multiple layers and involved processes is the way to go. Of course, to maintain the status quo in academia doesn't mean that no change will occur. It means that the system will continue to move in the same direction: toward more politicization.

If, on the other hand, you wish to address problems aggressively, it is best to instill a hierarchical form of governance with a clear chain of command. And with the trustees in charge. Only boards can represent all interests. And the American system of higher education was intended to function with boards in charge.

To preserve the best of higher education, something more fundamental—a "Copernican revolution," or "Kuhnian paradigm shift," if you prefer—is needed to turn academia back toward the spirit of open inquiry. Such a paradigm shift is called for when the existing framework is no longer sufficient to explain or solve existing puzzles; a new perspective is needed with greater explanatory power.

Such a shift in higher education would require reordering power relationships, elevating the power of governing boards, the public, and the alumni while reducing the power of faculty and administrators.

To many, such a recommendation may seem drastic, even alarming

Most commentary on higher education remains within fairly narrow boundaries; much of the best-known literature tends to be written by former college administrators, who have the seeming advantage of being "inside" the system, or else written by policy professionals from professional associations that have risen to prominence within the current system.

But their insider status also tends to blind them to the overall picture. They may decry the gridlock that an outside observer will perceive to be the natural result of shared governance, but they blame it on the governing boards, whom they would prefer to keep at a distance and forego their legal and natural authority. More faculty involvement, a more powerful administration, more shared governance is their solution.

But to support the current system is to permit antagonistic forces to incrementally dislodge the best of the Western intellectual heritage from the academy. This must not be allowed to happen!

Alumni Organize in Defense of College Free Speech

From the S.A.P.I.E.N.T. Being's *Free Speech Alumni Ambassador (FSAA) Program Handbook*, millions of college and university alumni around the country are dismayed by the intolerance of unpopular viewpoints at their alma maters, and now some have begun to fight back.

Alumni have organized groups at five of America's most prestigious higher-ed institutions—Cornell University, Davidson College, Princeton University, the University of Virginia, and the Washington & Lee University—to defend free speech, academic freedom, and viewpoint diversity on college campuses. Today these groups are announcing that they have joined forces under the banner of the Alumni Free Speech Alliance to launch a national effort to mobilize alumni.

"Free speech and academic freedom are critical to the advancement of knowledge and to the success of our colleges and universities," said Edward Yingling, a co-founder of the Princeton alumni group. "Yet these basic principles are under attack today at schools across the country."

National and school-specific polls show that high percentages of students and many faculty are afraid to express their views on controversial topics. In fact, discouraging numbers of students indicate in polls that free speech is not justified if certain groups find the ideas offensive. The Foundation for Individual Rights and Expression (FIRE) found in a survey this year that more than 80% of students report self-censoring their viewpoints at least some of the time, with 21% saying they censor themselves often.

College administrators and boards of trustees are often too timid to push back against the culture of intolerance on their campuses. Alumni have influence with college presidents and board members, who are constantly asking for their involvement and contributions. The five groups comprising the Alumni Free Speech Alliance share the conviction that alumni can create a countervailing force to stand up for free speech. The Alliance will promote the exchange of information and best practices between its member organizations and provide assistance to alumni at other universities who wish to create free-speech organizations and join the Alliance.

"American universities and colleges are entrusted with educating our youth to think critically, to explore all options, and to gain the skills needed for leading productive lives," said John L. Craig, president of Davidsonians for Freedom of Thought and Discourse. "This can be accomplished only in environments where the search for truth is unfettered. The forces against campus free speech and for ideological indoctrination are entrenched, and things can change only if alumni stakeholders strike back."

"Forty years ago, Cornell was a campus that embraced freedom of speech and great viewpoint diversity but the demographics of its student body and faculty were monolithic. Today Cornell enjoys great diversity within its student body and faculty but imposes significant barriers to freedom of speech and viewpoint diversity on campus," said Kenneth P. Wolf, co-founder of the Cornell Free Speech Alliance. "Neither of these extremes support academic excellence and, in the long run, will destroy a world class institution of higher learning."

"Conservatives, and increasingly liberals, are afraid to speak against "woke" orthodoxy at the University of Virginia," said Bert Ellis, president of the Jefferson Council. "The Jefferson Council was formed to preserve the legacy of intellectual freedom at the institution Thomas Jefferson founded. Core goals include the protection of free speech, free expression, and intellectual diversity."

"Education based on victimization, grievance, and critical race theory harbors the seeds of tribalism, cultural segregation, and erasure of

101

history," said Tom Rideout, president of the Generals Redoubt. "Conversely, education based on diversity of viewpoint and free speech promotes robust learning, the pursuit of truth, and an inclusive culture based on shared values."

Alumni Unite for Freedom of Speech

By now, you should be well aware that free speech, academic freedom and viewpoint diversity are in big trouble at U.S. universities. But many of those worried over the state of campuses are almost resigned to the idea that the forces of illiberal intolerance have won. The fight is far from over. On Oct. 18, 2021, five alumni groups announced the creation of an organization to stand up for open inquiry: the Alumni Free Speech Alliance (AFSA).

AFSA's founders are groups of graduates of Cornell University, Davidson College, Princeton University (our alma mater), the University of Virginia, and Washington and Lee University. Our allied organizations are the Cornell Free Speech Alliance, Davidsonians for Freedom of Thought and Discourse, Princetonians for Free Speech, the Jefferson Council (composed of UVA alumni) and the Generals Redoubt (W&L alumni).

AFSA's member groups are nonpartisan and will protect the rights of faculty and students across the ideological spectrum. The groups will pool ideas and information as well as promote and mentor similar groups of alumni from other schools. Our goal is to ally with scores of as-yet-unformed alumni groups around the country.

Why alumni? Because with rare exceptions, everyone else may feel too exposed to attacks to take a stand against campus culture. Our experience is that the few student free-speech groups don't have many members (Princeton's has about 20). Champions of free speech among faculty are badly outnumbered, even as many left-of-center professors are starting to realize that they too can be brutally canceled by the mob. Those few students and faculty who speak up often feel isolated and exposed.

University trustees, presidents and other administrators are also usually mired in the toxic campus environment, which responds to heresy with attacks. Most have either been cowed by or genuinely believe in a woke orthodoxy that sees free speech as an inconvenient disruption.

That leaves alumni as the only university stakeholders with the numbers and clout to lead the defense of free speech, academic freedom and viewpoint diversity in campus environments. Free speech and academic freedom are fundamental to the advancement of knowledge and to the success of our colleges and universities. Will all teaching and research at these schools soon be subject to a mandated orthodoxy? Will parents keep paying to send their children places where the fundamental elements of learning are suppressed? These institutions constantly seek alumni involvement and contributions. Alumni have the ability and duty to demand that their schools maintain the reasons for which they were created. But to be effective, alumni need to organize.

In a recent 2020 survey by the Foundation for Individual Rights and Expression (FIRE), more than 80% of students reported self-censoring their views at least some of the time, with 21% saying they censor themselves often. The survey, of more than 37,000 college students on 159 campuses, shows growing support among students for various forms of censorship, especially of conservative speakers, with 66% of students saying that shouting down speakers on campus may be justified. Other polls report similar results.

Tolerance for free speech among faculty appears to be marginally greater, but it is in decline; and left-tilted ideological litmus tests in faculty hiring have become common while moderate and conservative professors have become scarcer.

Hundreds of articles in numerous publications have reported on the harassment, suspension and even dismissal of faculty and students for expressing opinions, many quite reasonable, that offend woke activists. Meanwhile, university presidents often do nothing, even when their schools' free-speech rules would seem to require action.

Alumni—and that may include you—must act. Our five allied alumni groups stand ready to help.

About the Free Speech Alliance

Harvard Alumni for Free Speech is the eighth alumni free speech group to join the original five since the Alliance was announced on October 18, 2021. The previous new groups to join were from Bucknell, Lafayette, MIT, UNC, VMI, Wofford, and Yale. Since the announcement of the new Alumni Free Speech Alliance, we have been contacted by alumni from over 110 schools interested in forming alumni free speech groups for their schools.

We anticipate that many more such groups will join the Alliance in coming months.

The Alliance brings together alumni groups that have a focus on supporting free speech, academic freedom, and viewpoint diversity at their colleges and universities. The founding members of the Alliance were alumni groups from Cornell University, Davidson College, Princeton University, the University of Virginia, and Washington & Lee University, but other alumni groups are steadily joining the cause.

Members of the Alliance believe that free speech, academic freedom, and viewpoint diversity are critical to the advancement of knowledge and to very concept of a university. Yet surveys show most students at colleges and universities have little understanding of these principles. Most students oppose free speech. See, for example, the "2021 College Free Speech Ranking" published by the Foundation for Individual Rights and Expression (FIRE).

On many campuses, students and faculty are attacked for exercising free speech. According to the FIRE survey, over 80 percent of students at the schools surveyed said they self-censor in the classroom, on campus, and online.

To preserve the purpose of their institutions, alumni must become involved to make the case for free speech and academic freedom and to provide support for faculty and students who speak up on their campuses.

The Alliance provides a mechanism for the exchange of information among its members on substantive and organizational issues. A priority for the Alliance is to encourage the creation of alumni free speech groups for other colleges and universities, and the Alliance will create tools to help new alumni groups organize. We believe the number of alumni groups supporting free speech on their campuses will grow.

While members of the Alliance are alumni focused, other interested parties, such as faculty and students, may also be involved. Each of the members is different in terms of its organizational structure and activities but is committed to promoting free speech, academic freedom, and viewpoint diversity.

Listed below are the members of the Alumni Free Speech Alliance, with a click through to their websites:

- Bucknell: Open Discourse Coalition

- Cornell: Cornell Free Speech Alliance

- Davidson: Davidsonians for Freedom of Thought & Discourse

- Harvard: Harvard Alumni for Free Speech

- Lafayette: Alumni/Alumnae Coalition for Lafayette

- Massachusetts Institute of Technology: MIT Free Speech Alliance

- Princeton: Princetonians for Free Speech

- University of North Carolina: UNC Free Speech Alliance

- University of Virginia: The Jefferson Council

- Virginia Military Institute: The Spirit of VMI

- Washington & Lee: The Generals Redoubt

- Wofford: Alumni for the Wofford Way

- Yale: Fight for Yale's Future

How Alumni Can Organize to Support Free Speech and Academic Freedom At Their College or University

The members of the Alumni Free Speech Alliance (AFSA) encourage alumni from other colleges and universities to form their own organizations to support free speech, academic freedom, and viewpoint diversity at their institutions. Members of the Alliance are committed to providing resources and mentoring to assist with the creation of new alumni groups.

Alumni should realize that the future of their college or university could be at stake. Free speech, academic freedom, and viewpoint diversity are critical parts of the foundation of every college and university. If these core values are lost, your college or university will lose its very reason for existence. Many institutions may already be reaching a breaking point.

On many campuses, opponents of free speech and academic freedom are well-organized, while defenders of these values are not. Students and faculty who support these values often feel isolated and intimidated and do not speak up, even when they may be a majority. An organized group of alumni can advocate for free speech and academic freedom and provide much needed support for such faculty and students.

Each alumni group in the Alliance has its own structure and operates differently, but we share many common elements. Each of us started with a few dedicated alumni but grew quickly, as other alumni rallied to the cause. While forming a new group can seem daunting at first, the Alliance will be able to assist alumni who want to create new free speech organizations. We urge interested alumni to contact us through this website.

The Guiding Principles (Chicago Principles)

The mission of these alumni organizations is largely guided by the Chicago Principles, a declaration on free expression in academia originally developed by the University of Chicago. See the Resources section for a link containing more information.

After a series of incidents that "tested institutional commitments to free and open discourse," the University of Chicago established the Committee on Freedom of Expression in 2014 to write a statement articulating the school's dedication to ideological diversity.

To sum up the principles and push back against ideological censorship, the committee asserted that, "debate or deliberation may not be suppressed [on campus] because the ideas put forth are thought by some or even by most members of the University community to be offensive, unwise, immoral, or wrong-headed."

Supporting the free market of ideas, the Chicago Principles stated that, "It is for the individual members of the University community, not for the University as an institution, to make those judgments for themselves, and to act on those judgments not by seeking to suppress speech, but by openly and vigorously contesting the ideas that they oppose."

Following the creation of the Chicago Principles, a campaign arose to get them adopted on *other* college campuses. However, it wasn't until a few years ago that their implementation became a trend. Prestigious institutions like Columbia University, Claremont McKenna College, Vanderbilt University, and most recently, the University of Virginia have all endorsed Chicago's statement, and this was accomplished with significant help from concerned alumni.

This commitment to fostering debate and deliberation is an essential part of *any* university's educational mission because it challenges students to become articulate, independent-minded, critical thinkers. Traditionally, this has been the goal of higher education. However, in today's culture, that objective has been superseded by political agendas.

Say NO to Campus Mob Fascism With the Chicago Statement

In response to the Berkeley riot incident in 2017, the Foundation for Individual Rights and Expression (FIRE) issued this statement:

No university may be considered "safe" if speakers voicing unpopular ideas on its campus incur a substantial risk of being physically attacked. A university where people or viewpoints are likely to be opposed with fists rather than argumentation is unworthy of the name. Granting those willing to use violence the power to determine who may speak on campus is an abdication of UC Berkeley's moral and legal responsibilities under the First Amendment.

Strong-arming one's belief onto others is just a form of mob fascism—no matter what side of a political spectrum you are coming from. If the Chicago Principles support allowing any invited speaker, as the statement does, then great. We must value our wonderful educational space, framed by laws and policies on one side and supported by documents like the Chicago Principles on the other. We need students to feel free to offer any viewpoint and likewise to offer any challenge, both within the context of our curriculum and on campus, to open up a discourse, and to learn from the engagement.

Let's underscore that point at the beginning: the Chicago Principles envision and protect both controversial viewpoints and protests against those viewpoints, with the proviso that protesters "may not obstruct or otherwise interfere with the freedom of others to express views they reject or even loathe."

Any statement or policy that supports students' freedom of speech rights is welcomed. Below is an excerpt from the Chicago Statement as a reference if there is ever a question or push-back about allowing a controversial speaker on campus because someone finds some topic of inquiry distasteful.

"Because the University is committed to free and open inquiry in all matters, it guarantees all members of the University community the

*broadest possible latitude to speak, write, listen, challenge, and learn . . . .
[I]t is not the proper role of the University to attempt to shield individuals
from ideas and opinions they find unwelcome, disagreeable, or even deeply
offensive."*

The "Chicago Statement" refers to the free speech policy statement
produced by the Committee on Freedom of Expression at the University of
Chicago. In July of 2014, University of Chicago President Robert J. Zimmer
and Provost Eric D. Isaacs tasked the Committee with "articulating the
University's overarching commitment to free, robust, and uninhibited
debate and deliberation among all members of the University's
community." The Committee, which was chaired by esteemed University of
Chicago Law School professor Geoffrey Stone, released the report in
January of 2015.

Here are several tips for ensuring that your university will be the next
institution to stand in solidarity with the Chicago Statement's principles:

- Work to pass a student government resolution calling on the
  university to adopt its own version of the Chicago Statement.

- Reach out to faculty members and work with faculty governing
  bodies on campus.

- Build a broad coalition of students and groups, particularly across
  the ideological spectrum, to support the Chicago Statement and
  raise awareness on campus.

- Publish articles and op-eds in student newspapers and other
  outlets.

- Host events on campus, such as debates, speakers, and panels to
  discuss the principles supported by the Chicago Statement.

- Communicate and collaborate with members of your university's
  administration.

- Host a petition drive, asking students to pledge their support for
  the Chicago Statement's principles In a petition that will go to the
  administration.

8 – How to Defeat Left-Wing Radicalism by Protecting Free Speech Rights

From the Katrina Gulliver "Cancelling the Cancellers" *City Journal* October 2023 article covering the new FIRE book, *The Canceling of the American Mind: Cancel Culture Undermines Trust and Threatens Us All—But There Is a Solution*, by Greg Lukianoff and Rikki Schlott where Lukianoff considers how to upend the culture of fear on university campuses and beyond:

Greg Lukianoff, free-speech attorney, is back with a new book on the state of cancel culture. Lukianoff's previous book, *The Coddling of the American Mind* (co-written with Jonathan Haidt), addressed young people's emotional fragility and inability to handle conflict. In this new, similarly titled work, *The Canceling of the American Mind*, Lukianoff and coauthor Schlott turn their focus to the phenomenon of "cancellation": its origins, its corrosive effects, and how to push back against it.

Lukianoff and Schlott begin with a survey of cancel culture. They trace its origins to the anti-bullying movement, which told children to respond to bullying by telling an adult or a teacher about the mean kids. Proponents inculcated this approach among a whole generation. Those children have since grown up, and now, in the workplace, continue to "tell an adult" (in this case, their boss or HR) when conflicts arise.

Cancelling the Cancellers

Anyone born before 1985 likely grew up with a dim view of tattle-tales. (How many books and movies involve kids getting their own revenge on bullies by learning to fight back, and not involving any of the adults?)

The baby boomers saw the authorities as oppressive or irrelevant, to be ignored or rebelled against. Zoomers, by contrast, use the authorities as a dispute-resolution mechanism. In 1965, young people were sticking it to "the man"; in 2023, they demand that the man fire someone who uses a word they don't like on Facebook.

"The rise of Cancel Culture was not gradual," Lukianoff and Schlott observe. "On campuses across the country, it struck like lightning. Although students had long been generally supportive of free speech, a new generation of anti–free speech activists sprang up in the mid-2010s. Suddenly they were demanding speech codes, trigger warnings, and the policing of microaggressions."

The fuel of cancel culture is, of course, the power it gives to the cancellers. Teachers and professors can be canceled on the say-so of a motivated student. One shaky phone-camera video of a street argument can induce a life-changing hurricane of criticism that can escalate in some cases to ending a person's career.

We might be able to appreciate the thrill of turning the tables in a situation one finds unfair. And having complete strangers willing to jump in on your side? Power like that must be intoxicating. But that is an instinct we need to guard against, not just among the outrage-starters but also among those willing to join in, amplify, and validate the outrage.

The cancel crisis is not confined to America. "Although this book is focused on the United States," the authors write, "we will occasionally mention the insanity that has gone on in the United Kingdom, where hate speech laws can be deployed in service of Cancel Culture. In 2016 alone, more than 3,000 people were detained and questioned by police for non-crime 'hate incidents' related to what they had said on-line." This should terrify anyone who believes in free speech.

Cancel culture also can undermine public faith in institutions. Many institutions, responding to cancellers' pressure, have nailed their colors to one political mast and declared the other side the enemy. The authors highlight the pandemic as an example, when the public broadly got the message "that our institutions cannot be trusted to produce an accurate, unbiased body of shared facts."

Lukianoff and Schlott propose rolling back the cancel-culture tide with both attitudinal and organizational changes. They suggest banning political litmus tests at American universities, including "mandatory DEI statements and other attempts to select students or professors who hold a 'preferred' political viewpoint," and "any conservative equivalent" to such statements.

The authors also point out that, far from being a left-only tactic, cancel campaigns in education have been launched from the right, too. The administrations of most colleges and universities lean left, of course, yet cancel campaigns from the right are sometimes successful, and even those that aren't can lead to people being threatened and harassed.

On the structural side, the authors propose allowing students to test out of college altogether and move straight to graduate school. They also advise alumni to look at their alma mater's record on free speech and adjust their donations accordingly. Such changes may help to stem the cancelation avalanche. But economics is a factor, too: academia has too few jobs for too many candidates, thus making cancel campaigns driven by professional rivalry more likely.

By contrast, job-rich fields tend to see fewer cancellation attempts; accountants and oil rig engineers don't face social media pile-ons the way academics do. This reality may be harder to address.

Canceling is in some sections a rehash of *Coddling*; readers familiar with Lukianoff's work will likely be able to hum its main melody if not sing the chorus. The book's argument is sensible, and the authors are optimistic that change is possible. The greatest obstacle to ending cancel culture, however, lies in converting those who deny it exists or who believe its victims had it coming. The people who most need to read this book won't.

Speaking Up: A New Bill Offers Hope of Protecting Free-Speech Rights at American Universities

In the summer of 2021, North Carolina congressman Greg Murphy introduced the Campus Free Speech Restoration Act, designed to enhance free expression in American universities. Murphy's bill defines "expressive activities" to include peaceful assembly, speaking, and listening and protects them from "improperly restrictive" institutional incursions, such as speech codes, bias response teams, and "free speech zones."

That legislation of this kind might be necessary is a sad commentary on academia. But as observers of American higher education know, college is now a place where free inquiry, free speech, and intellectual growth are imperiled. Surveys show that many professors and students now self-censor for political reasons. A punitive progressivism has become dogma, and vague harassment policies, zealous students, and ideological administrators chill dissent. Laws such as Murphy's can help, but it's vital to get the details right.

Public universities, legally subject to the First Amendment, get away with unconstitutional practices when authorities fail to respect and enforce the law. This is because no constitutional provision is self-enforcing. To give it effect, an injured party must sue a school. But after filing suit, that party often endures years of "lawfare"—stonewalling, appeals, trials, re-trials, and remands—that public universities, with taxpayer funds and lawyers at their disposal, greet with a yawn. All too often, individual lawsuits against universities are simply pebbles thrown against the citadel.

Murphy's bill addresses this problem with two innovations. First, it authorizes the Department of Education to condition Title IV federal funding on First Amendment compliance at public schools. While the bill does not specify how this would be implemented, it could easily appear alongside longstanding requirements in each school's Program Participation Agreement, which requires that institutions refrain from discriminating based on race and sex. The condition could also be the subject of an independent, annual certificate of compliance filed separately by the school with the Department of Education. The certification would force schools to document their efforts to protect free expression and to record where and when it was threatened—whether in "shout-downs," intimidation of speakers resulting in rescinded invitations or canceled lectures—and to list measures taken to prevent such events from recurring.

Second, the bill creates a new position in the Education Department to oversee the status of free speech on campus and to enforce the First Amendment there, independent of time-consuming and expensive litigation. This official would investigate credible complaints of First Amendment threats and would be authorized to impose penalties in the event of noncompliance.

(The bill also conditions Title IV funding for private universities on disclosure and enforcement of free-speech policies. This imposition is less demanding since private schools are not bound by the First Amendment.)

While the bill is a good start, practical questions remain. Since the Department of Education's finding of noncompliance would remain reviewable by a court, does the bill's new federal review simply impose an extra bureaucratic layer on complainants? Won't this new Education Department official inevitably follow the policies of the administration in power? And, given that schools often cave soon after a complaint is filed by withdrawing contested policies—only to reintroduce the policies at a later date— how will the law prevent backsliding?

Modifications to the bill could account for some of these concerns. The legislation could further empower the Education Department position to conduct random audits on campuses to ensure that a school's culture, policies, and enforcement practices are First Amendment–friendly. The new office need not wait passively to receive complaints, but instead, like health and safety agencies, should proactively inspect premises to prevent injury.

The bill could also authorize the official to enjoin the problematic policy or action when a complaint makes a reasonable case of a likely violation. The burden of proof at this early stage would be intentionally low—in favor of the complaint and of free expression. This would help level the "lawfare" playing field, signal the importance of the First Amendment in the academic setting, and recognize the reality that institutions of higher learning no longer deserve the benefit of the doubt on speech issues.

Finally, the bill should require the Department of Education to notify a school's regents or trustees of any complaint, investigation, or injunction, as well as the associated costs. The board can then communicate with the general assembly to deduct such costs from the school's annual appropriations, which would, of course, be refunded or re-appropriated should a final judgment exonerate the school.

Taken together, these provisions would ensure that the institution bears the cost of likely constitutional violations—not the individual and not the taxpayers. More could be said about required elements for injunctive relief and about finding the right person to fill this new position. But with time and some tinkering, Murphy's legislation could be an important step toward rescuing American higher education.

Like the other proposed solutions in this section that address the freedom of speech and expression suppression taking place throughout America's educational institutions, the Free Speech Alumni Ambassador (FSAA) Program can be the catalyst to help make them happen.

How to Defeat Left-Wing Racialism

From the joint team of Wade Miller, Dan Morenoff, Ilya Shapiro, David E. Bernstein, James Sherk, Judge Glock, Christopher F. Rufo comes the article "How to Defeat Left-Wing Racialism" in the Summer 2023 *City Journal* reporting on a symposium on restoring the principle of color blindness brought together seven sapient scholars, researchers, and journalists together to collaborate on this insightful article and its action plan.

The summer of 2020 was a watershed in American life. After George Floyd's death in police custody and the ensuing season of rioting, major institutions—from federal agencies to Fortune 100 companies—hastily pledged themselves to the narrative of critical race theory, which holds that America is a fundamentally racist nation and that public and private entities should practice "antiracist discrimination" to equalize group outcomes—a state of affairs that its advocates call "racial equity."

This ideology stands in direct opposition to the principles of the Constitution, which provides for color-blind equality under law. Yet many American institutions quickly adopted "diversity, equity, and inclusion" policies, such as discriminatory hiring practices and racially segregated employee groups, that are, correctly interpreted, illegal.

We have convened a symposium with six of the nation's leading domestic-policy experts and asked them to consider how future policymakers might restore the principle of color-blind equality in government. Their recommendations are not comprehensive. But they would start the process—already begun, perhaps, by the Supreme Court's ruling that race-based college admissions policies are unconstitutional—of restraining the forces of left-wing racialism and moving the country back toward a regime of individual merit and fair treatment under law.

The article is by Christopher F. Rufo who is a senior fellow at the Manhattan Institute and the author of *America's Cultural Revolution*.

Defund the Left

The fight against a woke and weaponized federal government has begun, though it remains in its early stages. Wokeness in the federal government is best understood as a method of decision-making by activist bureaucrats. They determine how taxpayer money gets spent, who benefits, who loses, and which social-justice cause gets prioritized in government programming. Dismantling their taxpayer-funded supply lines is a critical element in defeating their efforts.

How to do this? For starters, Congress should continue to reduce nondefense discretionary spending and budget authority to pre-Covid levels—not just to curb inflation and bend the curve of the national debt but to reduce the power of the federal agencies and departments that have pursued agendas that stoke racial division.

A key component in the next budget fight should be ending competitive grant programs, most of which fund far-left organizations that use public money to advance their causes. The Appropriations Committee should turn off the competitive grant spigot altogether, or, at a minimum, include legislative and limitation riders that prohibit such funding from promoting divisive racialist theories.

The Rules Committee, meantime, should adopt new standards as part of the budget and appropriations process to forbid floor amendments that fund programs, agencies, or nongovernmental entities practicing diversity, equity, and inclusion (DEI). In tandem, lawmakers should consider more aggressive use of the Holman Rule, which lets House members cut specific programs and fire specific employees. This tool can be deployed to defund DEI departments and hold activist bureaucrats accountable to Congress.

Lastly, every House committee chairman should hold hearings that scrutinize the woke bureaucracies under their respective purviews. These congressional efforts will help build a public case against DEI and lay the groundwork for executive actions in a new administration.

The article is by Wade Miller who is a U.S. Marine Corps combat veteran who works in public policy.

Mobilize the Department of Justice Against Racialist Discrimination

An equality-friendly administration will need to prioritize its options for reversing the spread of racialist ideology across American institutions. Two initiatives should head the list.

First, the Department of Justice (DOJ) and other enforcement agencies should once again take seriously their obligation to ensure that our public and private institutions comply with Title VI of the Civil Rights Act and cease racial discrimination—including so-called antiracist discrimination based on critical race theory, which rewards or punishes individuals according to their racial identity.

To this end, the next administration should swiftly instruct all agencies to initiate investigations nationwide against entities that discriminate based on race and pursue cutting off federal funding for institutions that refuse to comply. Targets should include schools and universities and local and state governments. The Equal Employment Opportunity Commission should investigate corporations. The DOJ and EEOC should stand ready to follow through with litigation.

In education, this would mean probing many of the large school systems, including those in San Francisco, Boston, New York, and Northern Virginia, that have altered admissions policies to reduce the number of Asian Americans in magnet schools. Additionally, it would mean investigating many universities for discriminatory admissions policies (which the Supreme Court recently deemed unconstitutional) and racially segregated scholarships. University of Michigan professor emeritus Mark Perry has identified hundreds of these programs; all should be shut down.

Second, in partnership with the Securities and Exchange Commission and the Federal Trade Commission, the DOJ should investigate the three largest passive-investment firms—BlackRock, Vanguard, and State Street—for antitrust violations. These firms have aggressively promoted environmental, social, and governance (ESG) initiatives, which often encourage discriminatory racial quotas or segregated employee groups. Federal investigators should look for collusion in these firms' mutual participation in ESG activist initiatives and examine their lockstep adoption and advancement of parallel ESG goals.

As part of this investigation, the agencies should question the Clayton Antitrust Act's impact on these giant firms' joint control over vast swaths of the economy. Two of the "Big Three" are publicly traded—and the two largest owners of each are the other two, leaving the firms in apparent control of each other. The Big Three, jointly, are the largest shareholders in almost the entire S&P 500 stock-market index. They appear to hold joint control of 14 of America's 15 largest banks. If they are in violation of the Clayton Act, the government could force them to divest themselves from one another and bar them from colluding to promote adoption of discriminatory ESG policies. Good antitrust policy would be good civil rights policy.

These two initiatives would represent a starting point for reestablishing the government's commitment to equality for all.

The article is by Dan Morenoff who is executive director and secretary at the American Civil Rights Project.

Force Open Debate on Campus

Higher education is in crisis. Students and faculty are uncomfortable speaking their minds, lest they find themselves canceled; tuition costs are skyrocketing, far in excess of inflation; taxpayers are asking why they're paying for radical indoctrination.

This crisis is the result of an exploding university bureaucracy that subverts faculty governance in favor of an illiberal identitarianism. What began as administrative bloat has become a full-blown commissariat that stifles intellectual diversity, undermines equal opportunity, and excludes dissenting voices. The average four-year university now has more DEI officials than history professors. DEI offices have broadened the meaning of terms like "harassment" and "discrimination" not to promote a welcoming campus environment but to enforce progressive ideology.

How do we fix this mess? Appeals for internal reform aren't enough. The problem necessitates external controls from federal agencies, civil rights regulators, and congressional oversight, tied to federal funding.

Fortunately, Congress has already given the Department of Education (DOE) some tools to address these issues. The next administration should instruct the department to compel institutions to certify their compliance with federal requirements on the protection of student speech and association rights and with Supreme Court rulings that outlaw loyalty oaths. Just as all recipients of federal higher-education funds must certify compliance on everything from accounting standards to antidiscrimination practices, conservatives can mandate that they discontinue programs that undermine free speech and due process, as well as those that constitute compelled speech in the form of diversity statements.

Next, the Office of Civil Rights (OCR) should investigate any institution that admits to engaging in "systemic" or "structural" racism, as was claimed in so many self-flagellating statements three summers ago. In addition, to ensure that colleges and universities don't resist the Supreme Court's recent ruling that bans racial preferences in admissions, the OCR should require them to show that their admissions processes are indeed color-blind—whether by disclosing GPA and standardized test data, or by another method that prevents racial discrimination by proxy.

Finally, the DOE must overhaul accreditation metrics to focus on fraud prevention and academic rigor and must remove accreditation monopolies, such as the one that the American Bar Association enjoys over law schools, when institutions abandon (as the ABA has) their mission of neutral, merit-based judgment.

There's still a long way to go before higher education returns to its mission of seeking truth, but the next Department of Education has a vital role to play in advancing that process.

The article is by Ilya Shapiro who is a senior fellow and director of constitutional studies at the Manhattan Institute.

Roll Back Racial Classifications

In 1977, the federal government issued Statistical Directive No. 15, establishing America's official racial and ethnic classifications: black, white, Hispanic, Asian, and Native American. The purpose was to create uniform classifications, so that data for endeavors like civil rights enforcement and educational achievement could be shared and compared across government agencies. Nevertheless, the classifications quickly spread through American law and society and are now used for everything from college admissions to scientific research.

The problem: Directive 15 classifications are arbitrary and inconsistent, both in how they are defined and how they are enforced. The government developed its classifications through a combination of amateur sociology, interest-group lobbying, incompetence, inertia, and happenstance. The classifications never made much sense beyond the historical black–white divide. Now, given the country's dramatic demographic changes since 1977, they border on incoherence. It's time to reconsider them.

First, the next administration should review every instance in which the government uses, or requires private parties to use, racial classifications. These identity-group categories are inherently illiberal and divisive. Consistent with Supreme Court precedent, the government should get out of the racial-classification business entirely, unless a "compelling interest" exists for using such classifications.

Second, the administration should abolish the regulations that force biomedical researchers to classify their subjects and report data based on the Directive 15 classifications. These classifications have no plausible scientific justification; they absorb resources better spent on scientific advances; and they have stunted the development of therapies based on genetics.

Third, the next administration should reverse the Biden administration's plans to turn the Hispanic ethnic classification into a racial one and to add new Middle Eastern and North African (MENA) classifications. If implemented, both proposals would make our already-incoherent, arbitrary classification system even worse.

Fourth, to the extent that racial classifications do serve a compelling government interest, their use should be narrowly tailored to that purpose. One model to look at is the FBI's hate-crime statistics. The agency tabulates such crimes against 29 identifiable groups, among them Mormons and gender-nonconforming people.

Finally, to the extent that the Directive 15 classifications continue to be used, it makes sense, in many instances, to break up the broad, crude classifications into ethnic and national-origin subcategories. The "white" classification, for example, includes people with descent anywhere from Iceland to Yemen. "Asian" includes Bangladeshis and Filipinos. Limiting the data to the broad classifications, rather than digging deeper into their constituent parts, can obscure more than it illuminates.

The article is by David Bernstein who is a professor at the Antonin Scalia Law School and the author of *Classified: The Untold Story of Racial Classification in America.*

Balance the Federal Workforce—Intellectually

Some argue that civil rights laws can protect Americans from woke discrimination. That will not happen without significantly more viewpoint diversity in the federal bureaucracy. The federal workforce leans well to the left. Democrats outnumber Republicans about two-to-one. Headquarters employees live in an even more liberal environment: in Washington, D.C., Joe Biden took 93 percent of the vote.

In theory, civil servants' political views should not matter. In practice, conservative presidents frequently face internal resistance from long-serving bureaucrats with different political beliefs.

This is especially true in civil rights agencies. They naturally appeal to progressive activists who, once hired, systematically hire like-minded colleagues. During President Obama's first term, one DOJ Civil Rights Division (CRD) section almost exclusively hired left-wing activists into career positions.

This imbalance makes evenhanded enforcement of civil rights protections challenging. The woke employees who dominate the bureaucracy have no interest in combating woke discrimination.

For example, a DOJ investigation found that Yale University was discriminating against Asian and Caucasian applicants. Trump administration officials wanted to sue, but CRD career staff refused to participate in the litigation. The DOJ could bring charges only by using political appointees and detailing staff from other divisions. Career staff then dropped the case when President Biden took office.

Agencies have few political appointees; they rely on career employees for routine enforcement. Progressive domination of the career bureaucracy makes systematically enforcing protections against woke discrimination impossible.

The only solution is to increase intellectual diversity in the federal bureaucracy. Instead of focusing diversity initiatives on race or other protected characteristics, federal agencies should seek an intellectually balanced workforce. To achieve this, they should actively try to hire career employees whose worldviews differ from those of current staff.

In some departments, this might mean hiring more progressive employees. But in most, including the civil rights agencies, fostering intellectual diversity would mean recruiting and hiring more moderates and conservatives.

This can be done in several ways. The agencies could recruit new career staff from public-interest law firms like the Pacific Legal Foundation, Alliance Defending Freedom, and the Center for Individual Rights, or from red-state attorneys general offices. Similarly, they could proactively recruit graduates of conservative-leaning schools.

Federal agencies don't need a majority of their workforce to be conservative. They do need a critical mass of career employees who will enforce laws that activists on either side might oppose.

American society contains an enormous range of views. To a large extent, the career federal workforce—especially in civil rights agencies—does not. Until that changes, civil rights enforcement will not protect all Americans from discrimination.

The article is by James Sherk who is the director of the Center for American Freedom at the America First Policy Institute.

End Minority Contracting

The practice of favoring minority-owned firms in government contracts, though it does not get the headlines of affirmative-action plans in schools or workplaces, may have an even bigger impact. (See "Welcome to the World of Minority Contracting," Spring 2023.)

Federal, state, and local governments use "set asides" and no-bid deals to ensure that anywhere from 5 percent to 30 percent of their contracts go to minority businesses. Since nearly one-tenth of the American economy runs through government contracts, the consequences of these programs are significant. However, instead of righting historical wrongs, minority contracting has produced corruption and fraud, worsened racial tensions, and cost taxpayers billions of dollars.

We have lots of evidence that these programs encourage fraud. A 2016 Department of Transportation presentation stated that more than one-third of its contracting-fraud cases involved minority contracting. Whether it's construction at Chicago O'Hare International Airport, snow-removal deals in Atlanta, or casino projects in New York, minority-owned front companies often take a small cut and pass the work on to a white contractor, making a mockery of attempts to help the truly disadvantaged.

The result is significantly higher costs for taxpayers. Economist Justin Marion examined contracts on California highway projects before and after state voters banned racial preferences. Costs on the California projects dropped 5.6 percent compared with federally funded projects in which racial preferences remained in place. Studies of minority contracting show little or no positive effects on minority entrepreneurship.

How are these programs justified? In two cases, the Supreme Court said that governments could use racial contracting preferences only to remedy actual government discrimination. Instead of restraining such efforts, however, these cases spawned an industry for bogus "disparity studies" that legitimate them.

The solution is simple: Congress should end minority-contracting programs and ban the consideration of race (or sex) in all business decisions. As government continues to grow, Americans of all races don't want to spare ever more funds for ever worse service. They don't want their infrastructure projects sabotaged by costly requirements about the race of their contractors. And they don't want the government to enrich a small group of politically connected businesses that somehow get to claim the mantle of discrimination.

The article is by Judge Glock who is the director of research and a senior fellow at the Manhattan Institute and a contributing editor of City Journal.

9 – The Roadmap for Abolishing Racist DEI Programs & Bureaucracies

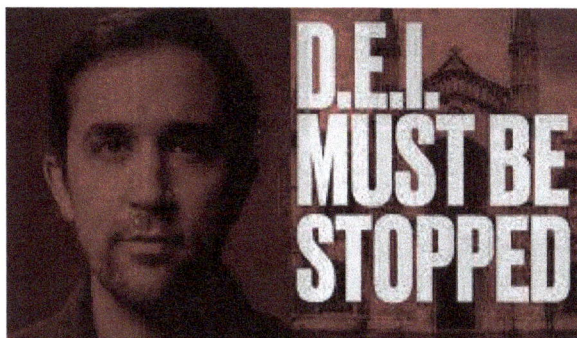

Credit: Manhattan Institute-"DEI Has Corrupted the Public Universities—And Must Be Abolished" video -by Christopher F. Rufo: https://www.youtube.com/watch?v=nw4BBQb71bg.

The public backlash to radical leftism opens opportunities for reform As noted in the Mike Gonzalez "Seizing the Moment" *City Journal* October 2023 article:

As it stands right now, America today is the closest it's been in a decade to recovering from its collective bout of racial and sexual hysteria. Conservatives must seize this moment and advance a policy agenda that could help the country emerge from this troubling period.

George Mason University senior research fellow Paul Aligica, who draws lessons from how "the institutionalization of indoctrination" (the title of his last book) was carried out in Eastern Europe, believes that Americans have a window of opportunity to stop those who want to reprogram the young in order to implement an "ideocratic" state. But that window, he warns, is closing. We need to keep it open.

Two recent events suggest that the United States might be at a turning point. First is the public's rejection of university students and their professors' justifying, or even celebrating, the recent massacre in Israel.

Seizing the Moment

Parents have been outraged by the reactions of their children's schools and used Facebook groups to organize in response, demanding, for example, that university presidents discipline or fire offending professors or administrators. Indeed, many parents now wonder whether those colleges' professors can be trusted to teach their kids. Donors are pulling their money from colleges that refused to condemn Hamas unequivocally.

Old-fashioned liberals drew the line when UC Davis professor Jemma Decristo publicly threatened violence against "[Z]ionist" journalists. More said "enough" after Cornell University history professor Russel Rickford called Hamas's carnage "exhilarating" and "energizing."

Humorist Bill Maher had a rational response that more accurately reflected the national sentiment. "There are few if any positives to come out of what happened in Israel," Maher said on his television show on October 20, 2023, "but one of them is opening America's eyes to how higher education has become indoctrination into a stew of bad ideas, among them the simplistic notion that the world is a binary place where everyone is either an oppressor or oppressed." Tragically, for some, it took a massacre of Jews in the Holy Land to spark such clarity.

A second event suggesting that America may be waking up to the excesses of wokeness was Ibram X. Kendi's recent fall from grace. Kendi's racialist worldview was inspired by a broader menu of Marxist concepts that have influenced American culture over the last 30 years. Less than four years ago, the *Washington Post* wrote that Kendi was "a leading voice among a new generation of American scholars who are reinvestigating—and redefining—racism." His ideas, another celebratory profile said, were "bracing and challenging." The *New York Times*, the *New Yorker*, and *The Atlantic* agreed. Former Twitter CEO Jack Dorsey gave Kendi a $10 million grant with "no strings attached."

After Kendi laid off 19 staff members at his Boston University center, leaving a much-smaller staff of 15, however, critics accused him of not producing any real scholarship, of having blown through at least $43 million, and of presiding over a toxic work environment.

Perhaps it should not be surprising that a man who wanted to create a federal Department of Antiracism, a nonelected body of technocrats that would approve or deny all new state or federal policy, would have authoritarian tendencies. Kendi's demand for unaccountable exercises of government power, coupled with his call for "future discrimination" to address past discrimination, should have made people think twice before backing him, but many critics kept silent, perhaps afraid of cancellation. Now, they're speaking out: BU is investigating Kendi, and his colleagues are acknowledging earlier misgivings.

"As one of a number of left-wing commentators who have been critical of mainstream anti-racism—and who believe the movement is little more than self-help for White people that runs interference for corporations and wealthy universities—I've watched the Kendi crisis unfold with a touch of schadenfreude," Tyler Austin Harper, a professor of environmental studies at Bates College, wrote in the Washington Post. David Decosimo, a BU colleague of Kendi's, put it even more sharply in the *Wall Street Journal*: "The debacle that is Boston University's Center for Antiracist Research is about far more than its founder, Ibram X. Kendi. It is about a university, caught up in cultural hysteria, subordinating itself to ideology."

Refreshingly (if only by current standards), both Harper and Decosimo still have their jobs. The one who has been put "on leave" is Derron Borders, the DEI director at Cornell, who posted, after the Hamas massacre: "Remember against all odds Palestinians are fighting for life, dignity, and freedom—alongside others doing the same—against settle colonization, imperialism, capitalism, white supremacy, which the United States is the model." Borders's example is useful in that it may lead more people to question why he was chosen in the first place to police the political views of students and peers, which is what DEI officers do. His outburst may open people's eyes to how DEI has been one of the main tools used to force-feed the "oppressed/oppressor" paradigm to students, with such effectiveness that it blinded many into defending mass killings and rape in Israel.

It's a propitious time, then, to take steps to rid our institutions of the DEI ideology. The White House and the Senate are in Democratic hands, making it unlikely that an anti-DEI agenda will get federal traction. Courts, though, can halt the institutionalization of DEI, such as forbidding federally funded institutions from compelling students to affirm ideological claims. Such indoctrination runs afoul of the Constitution's First Amendment protections against compelled speech.

This year 2024, of course, is a presidential election year, a prime opportunity to debate whether we want to continue on the current path of national and cultural self-destruction, or instead begin to free ourselves. If a new presidential administration takes office in 2025, it should formulate a clear plan for doing so, starting on January 20.

Meantime, much anti-DEI action can take place in state capitals. Most state 2024 legislative sessions start next January. Any state can confront the DEI problem, as Florida and Texas have already done in the realm of higher education. States should capitalize on the public's anti-DEI mood to enact policies safeguarding freedom of expression—particularly the freedom to reject lies that some have been forced to affirm, such as the notion that we live in a systemically racist society or that men and women can change their sex.

It should be illegal to demand that a person take a political loyalty oath as a condition of his graduation, employment, or promotion. This means supporting state efforts to make illegal any form of CRT, DEI, gender theory, or ESG that violates the Constitution. And until we have a new president who can do something about the mutilation of children in the name of "gender affirming care," or protect girls from having to compete against boys in sports or having to change in locker rooms with males who pretend they're female, states will have to take the lead here as well.

Policymakers also should start making the case against ethnic studies programs. As Evelyn Hu-DeHart, director of the Center for the Study of Race and Ethnicity in America at Brown University, put it, "Ethnic studies programs . . . challenge the prevailing academic power structure and the Eurocentric curricula of our colleges and universities.

These insurgent programs had a subversive agenda from the outset." Hu-DeHart helpfully makes clear what many people already suspected about such ideologically driven curricula. We should take steps accordingly to remove this content from our public schools.

And finally, it's time to consider investigating BLM and likeminded organizations. They're the ones who helped set the country on a path of collective mass hysteria when they were created in 2013, a process that greatly accelerated with the riots they encouraged and led in 2020. But BLM and its leaders have always been more about global revolution than about ameliorating the lives of black Americans, as they have made clear with their support for terrorism against Jews. Haul them into Congress and ask questions about their support for violent insurrection.

Investigate whether the more than 127 million emails the main BLM organization says that it sent in 2020, which led to "1,213,992 actions," had anything to do with the $1 billion–$2 billion in damage during the riots. Ask the leaders whether they want to bring down American society and implement a Marxist blueprint. It may be legal to do so peacefully; but put them on the record about what they believe and intend.

Recent events have demonstrated to the American public what wokeism, critical race theory, and the DEI agenda really mean. We may never have as promising an opportunity to push back against these ideas as we do now.

Giving DEI the Pink Slip

As per the Christopher F. Rufo "Giving DEI the Pink Slip" *City Journal* March 2024 article: Major institutions have started rolling back their diversity bureaucracies. Last year, conservatives began taking action against the "diversity, equity, and inclusion" bureaucracy.

The Manhattan Institute released a model policy to abolish DEI, exposed abuses in public universities, and advised political leaders, most notably Florida governor Ron DeSantis, in the crafting of legislation abolishing public-university DEI programs at the state level. To date, three states—Florida, Texas, and Tennessee—have passed laws abolishing or restricting DEI. A total of 17 states have either passed such laws or are considering them.

Our efforts are bearing fruit. Last week, the University of Florida, the flagship state institution, announced that it had dissolved its DEI department and terminated the employment of all DEI officials. UF was spending an astonishing $5 million per year on DEI programs, which university president Ben Sasse wisely redirected toward faculty recruitment. The new budget would presumably include recruitment for UF's Hamilton Center, a new home for conservative scholars. Sasse also offered a positive alternative to DEI, promising to hold the institution to the much better standard of "universal human dignity."

Conservatives are rightly celebrating the move as a watershed. DEI is not an inevitability; it is a choice that can be undone.

Corporate America is following suit. Firms including Google, Meta, and Zoom have quietly cut back DEI departments and laid off employees. I have recently spoken with a number of Fortune 500 executives, who explained that, following the summer of George Floyd, companies felt immense pressure to "do something" about racial disparities. But four years later, they have realized that DEI programs undermine productivity, destroy merit-based systems, and poison corporate culture. Because of our successful campaign to expose the true nature of DEI, they now have the political space—in essence, the social permission—to wind down these programs.

But we need to do much more. The best way to conceptualize DEI is as the marriage of ideology and bureaucracy, or, more specifically, as the marriage between critical race theory and affirmative action. On their path to power, DEI activists hijacked the Civil Rights Act of 1964—which, in spirit, enshrines policies of colorblind nondiscrimination—to justify active discrimination against supposed "oppressor" groups. In doing this, they have gained significant leverage. While the recent firings of DEI employees are a salutary development, the movement to restore colorblind equality can succeed only if we reform civil rights law to reinstate its original focus on individual rights under the law, without regard to race—and dramatically reduce the footprint of critical race ideologies in public universities.

That said, we should celebrate the moment. At the beginning of last year, when we formally launched the "abolish DEI" campaign, it was seen as a fringe, right-wing proposal. Since then, it has achieved significant political victories and become the mainstream position, with widespread support. While momentum is on our side, we should press for maximal demands: abolish DEI in all American institutions, terminate the employment of all DEI bureaucrats, and encourage them to find gainful work elsewhere.

Let us hope that this moment is only the beginning of a "pink slip revolution."

How Red-State Universities Evade DEI Restrictions

From the Scott Yenor "How Red-State Universities Evade DEI Restrictions" *City Journal* September 2023 article: Texas and Florida administrators in particular have devised end-runs around laws curtailing diversity, equity, and inclusion practices.

Even before the Supreme Court's ruling in Students for Fair Admissions, university administrators had begun adopting "holistic" admissions calculated to evade bans on affirmative action. But similar efforts to subvert state regulations on Diversity, Equity, and Inclusion (DEI) offices, policies, and activities have escaped public attention.

Legislatures in 22 states have proposed 40 bills to regulate DEI this year. Only seven have become law. Bills to curtail DEI activities in public universities have died in deep-red states like Ohio, Alabama, West Virginia, Louisiana, and Iowa. As of this past summer, at least five states (Florida, Texas, North Carolina, North Dakota, and Idaho) have banned the use of DEI statements in university hiring through legislation or administrative action. Two (Florida and Texas) prohibited the establishment of DEI offices; several others (including North Carolina, North Dakota, Tennessee, Texas, and Florida) have prohibited mandatory DEI training for employees.

Florida's and Texas's reforms stand out as the most impressive of 2023 to date. The Texas bill prohibits universities from operating offices that condone differential treatment of races, promote racial hiring, or conduct diversity training programs. Administrators who violate these provisions can be suspended after a first offense and fired after subsequent incidents. The Florida bill bans monies supporting DEI activities or political activism. Penalties for violations are enforced through administrative rules.

But while Texas and Florida universities are rewriting their rules to bring their practices into alignment with new state law, DEI commissars have signaled their intention to overcome the ban on DEI statements through "holistic hiring." Even as former Texas A&M president Kathy Banks was promising to obey Governor Greg Abbott's executive order banning DEI statements, her hand-picked associate provost for diversity, Annie McGowan, was articulating a strategy for obeying the letter of the law but violating its spirit. She told the Texas A&M Senate to discontinue DEI statements but to keep evaluating candidates based on their diversity-related experience and to construct job searches in such a way as to attract and hire DEI advocates.

Florida is still prepping regulations for dismantling DEI offices in public universities. Media reports suggest that the state's best academics and diversity advocates are being chased out. The reality is different: diversity advocates are, for the most part, disguising themselves and burrowing deep within bureaucracies to wait out the current political environment.

My 2023 report on Florida's university system showed that 13 public universities had upper-level DEI administrators. Ten of the 16 colleges at the University of Florida had dedicated DEI deans, while two were in the process of searching for deans. What has happened to these administrators under Florida law?

Three upper-level DEI administrators are no longer with their universities, while one has remained with the university, albeit in what legitimately seems to be a different position. Upper-level DEI administrators have left the University of Florida and Florida Atlantic University for DEI positions at other universities. The New College chief has left the school. The other switched roles from chief diversity officer at the University of South Florida-St. Petersburg to director of strategic accreditation initiatives.

Most Florida universities have not changed, however. Two higher-level administrators remain in office with new DEI titles. The University of West Florida's chief diversity officer, for instance, is now associate vice president for academic engagement and chief diversity officer. But a number of public universities have kept their DEI administrators in place. The University of North Florida still has a chief diversity officer, while the University of Central Florida still has a vice president for diversity, equity, and inclusion, and Florida International a vice provost for DEI. Florida Gulf Coast University still has a chief equity, ethics & equity officer and Title IX coordinator.

A similar pattern exists at the dean level at the University of Florida (UF), where five colleges have either kept their deans unchanged or given them slightly different titles. In nursing, the associate dean for diversity, inclusion, and engagement is now the associate dean for community engagement and global affairs. Another went from being the assistant dean for inclusion to the assistant dean for experiential learning and engagement in the Levin School of Law. No changes have been made in the job descriptions of any of the six deans of "community and belonging" in UF's School of Medicine; nor have there been changes for the associate dean for belonging in the College of Pharmacy or the assistant dean for community building and engagement in the College of Veterinary Medicine.

Texas administrators are showing similar defiance to the state legislature. Both Texas and Florida affiliate with the Hanover Research Group, which cites DEI as a core value, for the provision of faculty training. Cara Crowley, vice president of strategic initiatives at Amarillo College, works with Hanover. In a recent webinar, she shared "different approaches" her college is using to get around Texas's law, including rebranding DEI as "Love Your Neighbor."

"We are trying to focus the attention back on the work," Crowley explained, "and take politics out of it, but make it everybody's job. Whether you are staff or you're the president of the college, we all have a commitment to racial inclusivity."

University administrators no longer talk of political activism but instead emphasize personal self-help, safety, and relieving stress. Advocates avoid DEI language and instead use terms like "belonging." Colleges in Texas can work around state law by moving money around to make DEI efforts seem private or federal rather than state-driven. In Crowley's words: "We are higher ed. We all have work arounds."

State regulators need to be savvy to these deceptions. Lawmakers should consider stiffer penalties and broader implementation to avoid the game of Whac-a-Mole that college and university administrators want to play. Ultimately, personnel is policy, and universities need new leaders who will adhere to both the letter and the spirit of these state laws.

Harvard Alums Run Outsider Campaign to Overhaul Presidential Selection Process, Eliminate DEI

This article courtesy of Caroline Downey "Harvard Alums Run Outsider Campaign to Overhaul Presidential Selection Process, Eliminate DEI" at *National Review* on January 31, 2024 reveals the following:

Growing up in South Africa, Julia Pollak, a 2009 Harvard graduate, was warned against attending college in her home country. Frequent violent protests would force the local university to close for weeks at a time. The school plummeted in international rankings. Appointments to the administration were based on two criteria: "race and connection to the ruling party," Pollak told *National Review*.

"That university had forgotten its academic mission," she said. "Those politics and complete obsession with rapid racial transformation of the faculty as its guiding star. As a result, it allowed merit and the ordinary function of the university to get destroyed."

Pollak's mother, who sat on the boards of two South African universities, urged her to find a college abroad that valued intellectual freedom. In 2005, that's what Harvard was.

"When I got there, there was still tremendous viewpoint diversity among the faculty," Pollak said. "You could hear Cornel West calling for socialist revolution in one class and Harvey Mansfield calling for a return to classical values in another."

Now, Pollak is concerned that Harvard is heading down the same path as those hollowed out universities she left behind in her home country. Since the recent resignation of former Harvard president Claudine Gay, following scandals of campus antisemitism and plagiarism in her past scholarship, prominent alumni have demanded reform.

Harvard University's chief DEI officer, Sherri Ann Charleston, was also recently accused of plagiarizing 40 times in her academic work, such as her dissertation and a journal article, using other scholars' writing without proper attribution, according to a complaint obtained by the *Washington Free Beacon*.

The "Renew Harvard" four want Harvard to revive the commitment to academic excellence that made it famous the world over.

But to effect change, you need to infiltrate Harvard's fortified bureaucracy, where diversity, equity, and inclusion still reigns, despite Gay's departure.

Cue: the "Renew Harvard" slate.

Four Harvard graduates dedicated to restoring the university's commitment to open debate are running for seats on Harvard's Board of Overseers, the school's second most powerful governing body, which sits under the Harvard Corporation. The board of overseers acts as a check on the smaller Harvard Corporation and, crucially, has a role in confirming the individual selected to succeed Gay as president of the university. Certain members of the board will likely serve on the presidential search committee, the Harvard *Crimson* reported.

"The previous selection process was conducted in record time," Pollak said of Gay's selection. "It appears, though, the important questions were not asked. This time around, we will be asking all the uncomfortable questions. Is this the most qualified candidate? Is this candidate's publication record high quality enough?"

Though it has minimal formal powers, the board has major responsibilities and the ability to impact the academic direction of the university.

But unless Pollak, Zoe Bedell, Logan Leslie, and Alec Williams get seated on

132

the board, the status quo is unlikely to change. The graduates must each receive 3,238 alumni nominations by Wednesday to make it onto the ballot for the spring's election. As of Sunday, they collected 1,500 signatures, according to business mogul Bill Ackman. In recent months, Ackman, an old-school Democrat and Harvard alum, has published his revelations about DEI and promised to put financial weight toward its destruction in academia. He also endorsed the "Renew Harvard" candidates.

The barrier to entry to the 30-person Board of Overseers used to be a lot lower for outsiders like this year's four petition candidates, Bedell said.

Only 600 signatures were once required to get on the ballot if you weren't selected by the Harvard Alumni Association, at which point all Harvard alumni have the opportunity to vote. But a successful petition process in 2020 ended in five candidates being nominated and three getting elected to the board.

"After that, they changed a bunch of the rules," Bedell said. "Now you need 3,200+ nominations. They also capped the number of 'petition candidates' who can actually serve on the board to six total."

The Harvard Alumni Association is running their own roster of eight pre-approved candidates who match the tone of the last couple decades. DEI was woven throughout an online Q&A in *Harvard Magazine* featuring the eight candidates.

One candidate, a former president of the Harvard Alumni Association, wrote that a key campus priority for Harvard must be: "Remaining true to our values of diversity, equity, and inclusion, and showcasing how including people from a wide range of backgrounds can enable everyone to thrive."

Another candidate said, "Throughout my career and participation on numerous boards, promoting DEI (Diversity, Equity, and Inclusion) and cultivating leadership have been driving principles and commitments. I have witnessed the adverse impacts that result from racism in healthcare and academia, and am committed to advancing the mission of fostering access to the transformative power of higher education for the benefit of all."

As it stands, even if all four of the "Renew Harvard" contenders are the four highest vote getters in the race, only the top two will be seated. The other spots go to the alumni association candidates, who, while professionally accomplished, are likely to keep the school mired in DEI.

"There's an institutional pressure there," Bedell said. "That's where most of the candidates have come from. We're in the situation that we're in today so that suggests that it's not a process yielding people who have concerns about where things stand today."

Typical board elections are uneventful but not particularly transparent, with low turnout and most of the process happening behind closed doors, Leslie said. But he believes his team could have significant influence if they're elected in spite of the procedural roadblocks.

"Under the old regime, we'd all be on the ballot already," he said. If Harvard wants to restore its reputation, it has to get out of politics, the four "Renew Harvard" candidates argue.

The group is advocating for the University of Chicago standard, or a policy of neutrality on political matters paired with a firm dedication to free speech for students and faculty. Harvard's response to October 7. 2023, and its aftermath was predictable, as parroting the progressive line has been its routine for many years. But this time, it backfired, Leslie said.

While donors rarely threatened to withdraw in the past, October 7 was a "tremendous wake-up call." Harvard reacted the way it normally did in these types of fraught situations, "but this time it came under an immense kind of scrutiny."

"It doubled down on their errors and hopefully it reset the tolerance I think people have for the institution to act the way it has been acting," Leslie said.

Suddenly, Harvard's folly was exposed for the world.

"If Harvard had upheld a standard where it does not take positions on social issues, then it would not have taken all sorts of positions on race and racism over the last decade or more, but it did," he said. "Therefore, there was an expectation that Harvard would take a position on issues of the day. When the 34 student groups issued their statement, . . . [a] ridiculous, highly offensive statement, Harvard just melted away."

"Instead of reassuring the world that it stands against antisemitism, stands against terrorism, stands against genocide, stands against all these things, it didn't," he continued "It shirked away. You saw the former president kind of melt in front of the scrutiny, in front of Congress, then trying to retreat into a neutral, contextual stand, which is deeply inconsistent with how Harvard has treated every other issue."

The coddling of progressive students in recent years made Gay's testimony and the university's tolerance for antisemitism all the more galling, Pollak explained.

"I think it's made some egregious decisions, like removing Dean Ron Sullivan from his deanship because he joined Harvey Weinstein's legal defense team because a lot of students said it made them feel unsafe," Pollak said. "And yet, they're not protecting students on campus from speech that should actually make you feel unsafe," she said, presumably referencing the anti-Jewish hatred sweeping the Ivy League in recent months.

"It's an unequal enforcement of the rules and there's sort of a tragedy in the political climate of fear and conformity."

Overall, the four petition candidates are urging accountability and a higher standard of leadership at Harvard.

The head sets the tone and the agenda, Pollak said. Pollak recalls Gay's statements about the Supreme Court decision that struck down affirmative action in college admissions. Her email to the student body called the day "a tragedy" for the community, assuming everybody on campus was mourning.

"That kind of posturing is completely inappropriate," Pollak said. "The head of the university must assume that there are multiple different views among students, among faculty, and must create space for their views to be heard and seen as legitimate. You can't delegitimize half the country. It definitely starts at the top."

Pollak hopes the rigorous intellectual life she remembers at Harvard can be restored. Coming from the political Left, she had never been exposed to conservative ideas until she came to the school in the early 2000s.

"Being able to study with Niall Ferguson and Harvey Mansfield and Ruth Wisse, these great conservative intellectuals with whom I argued and fought," she said. "It was delightful and delicious and a fabulous education."

Most of those legends have retired and have not been replaced, she added. Over 80 percent of Harvard faculty describe themselves as "liberal," according to a July 2022 *Harvard Crimson* survey. The lack of conservative faculty is not accidental, Pollak said, because the people who are choosing professors are not seeking true diversity in their hires.

"The departments perpetuate themselves and their own ideas," she said. The commencement speaker rosters are embarrassing. They always look like a Democratic Party convention."

For an informative video about this topic, please check out the Appendix for "DEI Has Corrupted the Public Universities—And Must Be Abolished" by Christopher F. Rufo from the Manhattan Institute.

10 – Tomorrow's Woke Free Colleges Made Possible by Today's Woke Busters

Credit: Daniel A. Varela/Miami Herald via AP - Florida Gov. Ron DeSantis signing of HB7, "individual freedom," also dubbed the "stop woke" bill on April 22, 2022..

Enough is enough! Our colleges and universities should redeem the promise of the new academic year by reaffirming their commitments to freedom of expression. But for most it doesn't happen and the telos of truth has been replaced by social justice.

Long after alumni leave campus, they remain some of higher education's most powerful constituents. So why do we continue to faithfully donate to our favorite colleges year after year when they suppress freedom of speech, restrict academic expression, and prohibit viewpoint diversity? Or worse, perpetuate cancel culture, woke ideologies, and divisive DEI policies? Is that what you're funding?

Just how oppressive is the university environment when it comes to free expression with our woke educational institutions? More than 80% of students said they self-censor at least some of the time on campus, according to a recent survey by RealClearEducation, College Pulse, and FIRE, which covered more than 37,000 students enrolled at 159 colleges.

Why Campuses Need a Free Speech Alumni Ambassador (FSAA) Program

Censorship in the academic community is commonplace. Students and faculty are increasingly being investigated and punished for controversial, dissenting or simply discomforting speech. It's time for colleges and universities to take a deep breath, remember who they are and reaffirm their fundamental commitment to both free speech and freedom of expression.

How Do We Define Freedom of Expression?

Freedom of expression is the ability to decide for one's self what one wants to say, what one wants to believe and be able to communicate that with others. That's a very broad definition.

There are lots of ways in which we see limitations on freedom of expression that sometimes might be appropriate. But it's important to think about it broadly, to think about it as taking a lot of different forms, and to think about it specifically within the context of human beings' own ability to define for themselves what truth is.

People started saying "freedom of expression" several decades ago in part because when people would say "freedom of speech," that was mostly about actual talking and about expression of opinions. People started moving towards the term "freedom of expression" because it became very clear that acknowledging the expressive element of what you wear, what signs you carry, what arm bands you wear was a way of making the point that a lot of what we think the founders would've thought of as freedom of speech is much broader than just spoken words.

The **Free Speech Alumni Ambassador (FSAA) Program** helps create faculty and administrative positions, throughout America's predominantly liberally staffed college campuses, that can serve as much needed conservative club advisors—because conservative students are facing many obstacles when they attempt to start and charter a right-leaning student organization on campus due to faculty members fearful of losing their jobs or tenure for becoming these organization's advisors.

As campuses grow more hostile to free expression, it seems more apparent that it may be up to alumni to tip the scales in favor of individual rights. Long after alumni leave campus, they remain some of higher education's most powerful constituents. Now, with help from the Foundation for Individual Rights and Expression (FIRE) and the newly launched Alumni Free Speech Alliance (AFSA), they are beginning to rise up on behalf of free speech.

The FIRE is a nonpartisan, nonprofit organization dedicated to defending and sustaining the individual rights of students and faculty members at America's colleges and universities. These rights include freedom of speech, freedom of association, due process, legal equality, religious liberty, and sanctity of conscience — the essential qualities of liberty.

The AFSA, composed of five independent alumni groups from top institutions, seeks to "encourage the creation of alumni free speech groups for other colleges and universities," provide the "tools to help new alumni groups organize," and support "free speech and academic freedom." These groups will pool resources and mentor emerging alumni groups at other schools as they seek to establish themselves.

A key component to ensuring this happens is by developing and funding a FSAA Program at all educational institutions.

Alumni Are the Key

The Foundation for Individual Rights and Expression (FIRE) has been working with AFSA and many of the member groups over the past few months and is proud to partner with them to give alumni a real, independent voice for free speech on their campuses.

Per the "Alumni Take Up the Fight for Free Speech—and You Can Help!" Connor Murnane FIRE October 21, 2021 report: American universities routinely rely on their graduates for everything from word-of-mouth endorsements to checks that support the endowment. And yet even with confidence in higher education falling, year after year, alumni have been more than willing to give back.

A Council for Advancement and Support of Education report published in 2020 found that alumni contributed more than $11 billion to their alma maters in 2019. Alumni generosity not only helps keep colleges afloat, but also influences universities' placement in the *U.S. News and World Report's* annual college rankings — an important metric for university administrators and incoming students. Alumni have the opportunity to leverage this influence to ensure their schools uphold their obligations to the highest principles of free speech and academic freedom.

The fight to stem the tide of illiberalism on campus must be fought at every level. As the AFSA notes, "opponents of free speech and academic freedom are well-organized." More than that — they're institutionalized. It is time for the alumni proponents of free speech to organize as well and begin demanding these few, simple solutions that will build a culture of free expression on campus:

1. Demand your institution live up to its First Amendment obligations or commitments to free expression. Insist your institution's administration review campus policies and reform policies that restrict speech in ways that satisfy various campus missions while also respecting the individual rights of students and faculty.

2. Advocate for the adoption of the Chicago Statement on Freedom of Expression. When students see the leaders of their schools publicly pledge to protect free expression, they feel more secure to speak their minds. That also sets an important expectation for prospective students: Come to campus ready to participate in a free exchange of ideas. For more info on the Chicago Statement on Freedom of Expression please read further.

3. Insist your alma mater instills values of free expression from day one. It is clear that colleges cannot expect students to arrive on campus with knowledge about the importance of free speech and academic freedom, and this is leading to a profound mismatch between some students' expectations and the reality of a liberal education. FIRE's Freshmen Orientation Program consists of a series of modules that provide colleges with the materials necessary to teach the importance of free speech and academic freedom, which they may freely use and adapt to their own needs.

4. Insist your alma mater collect serious data on campus censorship and openness toward free expression. Every institution of higher education should remain vigilant about potential threats to free speech and gather information about its campus climate instead of simply claiming, "Other schools are like that, but not mine!" A transparent survey of a large proportion of the campus community can provide vital information that would allow administrators to

make informed decisions. If done annually, it could be used to judge yearly progress toward a free and open campus climate.

5. Stop writing blank checks. Alumni must begin focusing their financial investments in their alma maters toward liberty-oriented initiatives that will benefit the state of free speech on campus. Donations can have a much greater impact on the campus climate if they are earmarked toward scholarships, speaker series, independent academic programs, student groups, or other, non-general fund programs that encourage open dialogue and debate.

6. And finally, create a full time Free Speech Alumni Ambassador (FSAA) Program or Alumni Free Speech Alliance (AFSA) group. Both can advocate, facilitate, and manage a campuses commitment to freedom of speech and expression as well as ensure conservative campus organizations can be chartered on campus knowing they can partner with an advisor who will meet the college's minimum requirements for becoming an approved organization on campus.

Without dedicated FSAA personnel on campus and an AFSA group to champion a university's commitment to freedom of speech and expression, the counter prevailing forces will return the status quo orthodoxy and business as usual to the detriment of the marketplace of ideas, viewpoint diversity, intellectual humility, and the pursuit of free speech and freedom of expression.

Mission and Vision Statements

Create an alumni driven AFSA group and alumni association approved FSAA Program throughout America's college campuses to ensure that all educational institutions live up to their obligation of free speech and freedom of expression—for all.

Fulfill a university's commitment to freedom of speech and expression so that all campus organizations, regardless of their ideology, can partner with a campus advisor, and flourish and prosper—safe in their first amendment rights—united in their pursuit of the telos of truth.

Starting a Free Speech Alumni Ambassador (FSAA) Program on Campus

Because conservative students are facing many obstacles when they attempt to start and charter a right-leaning student organization on campus due to faculty members fearful of losing their jobs or tenure for becoming these organization's advisors—the Free Speech Alumni Ambassador (FSAA) Program was started to help create faculty positions at America's predominantly liberally staffed college campuses, that can serve as much needed conservative club advisors.

The population served by the Free Speech Alumni Ambassador (FSAA) Program are students, faculty, alumni, and trustees and the program intends to solicit funding, if available, to staff an independent Free Speech Alumni Ambassador to help ensure that free speech, viewpoint diversity, intellectual humility, and critical thinking (sapience) are protected on campus.

Per Corey Lee Wilson, CEO of the S.A.P.I.E.N.T. Being, the FSAA Program is currently in the process of requesting from American colleges and universities that the FSAA Program be announced, and recorded in the meeting minutes, at their next student government meeting for consideration and implementation on their campus.

For a brief introduction to the FSAA Program, please check out the Executive Summary below.

Free Speech Alumni Ambassador (FSAA) Program

Higher education is approaching an existential crisis. It is in danger of rejecting its most fundamental value, the search for truth, and replacing it with political dogma and opportunistic careerism. Other problems abound, but none so serious as this one.

In a well-run higher education system based on the honest pursuit of truth, the marketplace of ideas would permit critics to attack, refute, and even satirize such ideas.

The worst theories would be prevented from gaining even a tiny foothold; the rest would be condemned to some musty little corner while more reasoned ideas displaced them. But that is not the case; the free market of ideas is broken, replaced by a one-sided, dogmatic consensus.

In much of the humanities and social sciences, political dogma has already replaced objective inquiry. In some schools of education, for example, science is considered dependent upon the background of the individual instead of having universal principles for all, with indigenous myths considered equal to rigorous research methods.

How Can This Be Happening In Plain Sight, Without Spurring A Massive Campaign For Reform?

It's been evident for some time now throughout America's public and private educational institutions, that academia no longer promotes a culture that inspires courageous collaborations, free speech, and free expression, allows people to peacefully exchange ideas and meaningfully engage with people who have differing views. Nor does it place telos (truth), logic, and critical thinking over ideological and social justice initiatives.

Two conditions are needed to effect large-scale reforms in academia to address these problems:

- A hierarchical, top- down system of governance that can enact sweeping changes.

- And for that system to be controlled or heavily influenced by those outside the system.

These are two of three objectives of the Free Speech Alumni Ambassador (FSAA) Program.

Bolstering the Board: Trustees and Alumni Are Academia's Best Hope for Reform

In congruence with the Free Speech & Peace Research Grant's goal of embracing differences, the FSAA Program's alumni ambassadors and their trustee constituents can lead the way towards new ideas and innovations that improve campus governance in regards to protecting freedom of speech and expression, revaluating existing ideological orthodoxy, as well as enlightening academia, administrators, and students to alternate points of view throughout the marketplace of ideas.

Strong board governance provides immediate remedies for all these illiberal and irrational conditions. Most university boards, especially the public ones, were created by charters or statutes that placed the board fully in charge, and, remarkably, the boards legally retain much of their power. And yet, because of a variety of pressures and distortion, most boards have relinquished their rightful positions atop college and university governance.

Nonetheless, it may be that much of higher education is beyond reform. Having the will to reform is imperative; without that, nothing will drive change. Most elite private schools appear to have reached the point of no return. They are insulated from change by large endowments, tradition, and terminal groupthink; the politicization has metastasized, and only some unforeseen act of creative destruction will cause a reversal.

In such a scenario, the first place to look at the root of the problem is governance policies and practices. An examination of such practices reveals a system of "shared governance" that is guaranteed to prevent bold leadership at the top. Furthermore, shared governance and other academic cultural practices that give authority to mid-level individual employees and other bureaucrats prevent almost any attempt to right the ship of institutional state.

Reform Cannot Be Expected To Happen In A Broad-Based, Organic Fashion From Within

The incentives are such that those who see the need for reform put their careers in peril for speaking out. The psychological phenomenon known as "groupthink" is creating a dangerous uniformity in many departments and disciplines.

The reason is that the governance of academia has become almost terminally sclerotic and self-interested; academic leaders simply cannot, or will not, respond to these destructive trends. The results are appalling— but it doesn't have to be this way.

To help return governing to the board, the FSAA Program is intended to operate on two levels. One is to make the case for stronger board control. Such a hierarchical system, rather than the distributed shared governance system that exists now, is necessary to effect large-scale reform.

The FSAA Program also works on a more immediate, pragmatic level, providing proven solutions like adopting the Chicago Principles that can be implemented bilaterally to begin the process of reforming governance that effects freedom of speech and expression. In most situations, boards still have extensive legal authority, they merely need to exercise their existing authority, to put the brakes on many of academia's free speech suppression.

Educating Students About the Value of Free Expression, Open Inquiry, And Civil Discourse

Furthermore, as a third objective of the FSAA Program, there needs to be sustainable and ongoing undergraduate programming that models civil discourse, open inquiry, and educates students about the value of free expression. Indeed, in many departments on many campuses—the spirit of free and open inquiry is under attack.

Irrational theories, such as the belief that race and gender are mere social constructs, are proliferating. Political correctness and corporate and government money are distorting scientific exploration.

Many departments are dominated by adherents of fundamentally flawed philosophies, such as post-modernism or today's progressivism. Disturbed or hostile individuals are routinely hired, while conservative scholars "need not apply" to many departments.

On occasion, even political liberals who express moderate views in public are hounded out of their jobs.

All of this needs to stop before it is too late to enact much needed changes.

Additional Information and FSAA Program Handbook

For a deeper dive into our FSAA Program, the S.A.P.I.E.N.T. Being has published a 60-page handbook that can be accessed online at https://www.sapientbeing.org/programs. For immediate questions and requests for additional information, please contact Corey Lee Wilson by phone at (951) 638-5562 or email him at sapientbeing@att.net and he'll get right back to you.

Regarding the Society Advancing Personal Intelligence & Enlightenment Now Together (S.A.P.I.E.N.T.) Being; it was founded in 2019 as an educational 501 (c) (3) non-profit organization and non-political think tank, EIN 83-3685019, has a GuideStar Silver Rating, an active Board of Directors, and a website at www.sapientbeing.org.

College of the Future

The University of Austin (UATX) is happening—and it will help rescue American higher education as announced in the Jacob Howland "College of the Future" *City Journal* Winter 2023 article:

By almost any measure, colleges and universities are failing students—and the country. They provide an increasingly inferior product at an increasingly exorbitant cost. It's a joke that many universities have more administrators than undergraduates. It's a huge problem that only a third of all college students expect that they will be prepared to enter the workforce when they graduate, and that employers nevertheless believe that recent graduates vastly overrate their competencies. It's a scandal that fewer than 60 percent of students who enroll in a four-year college graduate after six years, and that many of these—not to mention those who do obtain a degree—leave with crippling debt. But the failure of our universities imperils more than the economy. It has damaged our essential institutions and has begun to erode the foundations of civilization itself.

Education joins what would otherwise be separated, enlarging the realm and enriching the comprehension of human experience. It works in multiple dimensions, linking past and future, time and eternity, and the individual with society and the world. The person mired in ignorance is disconnected from what is before and after, above and below, and from his neighbor on either side, like a point frozen at Cartesian coordinates (0,0,0). This is the situation of the prisoners in Plato's Cave, who, in their media-saturated ignorance, are chained by the neck so that they can see nothing of themselves or their neighbors and nothing above or behind them—nothing but shadows that flash before their eyes.

The backbone of civilization links the discernible past with the uncharted future. But the civilizational spine that gives form and spiritual firmness to a nascent age does not grow spontaneously. It is generated and regenerated by education, which preserves and transmits the hard-won inheritance of tradition and culture. In receiving this multifaceted inheritance, we come to appreciate the necessary conditions of peaceful order and human flourishing. And in encountering the best—and honestly acknowledging and wrestling with the worst—that has been thought and said and done, we learn to look up and around: to search out timeless truth and transcendent being and to attend to our neighbors. Thus enlarged, we may at last become capable, as John Henry Newman wrote in *The Idea of a*

University, of forming an "instinctive just estimate of things as they pass before us."

The word "education" comes from the Latin educare, "to lead out" or "to bring up." Many American colleges and universities, however, approach education in ways that effectively keep students down. They teach them that our aspirations for truth, beauty, and goodness have been mere projections of the lowest instincts: instruments of domination and servitude, power, and systemic injustice—as though there were nothing beyond the rigged game of the Cave, where a few puppeteers keep multitudes of oppressed peoples in the dark. That teaching would be unobjectionable, were the voices opposing such reductivism as audible on campus as those advancing it. But they are not.

What is strange is that many professors accept the puppeteers' terms, even as they rail against them.

They act as if their job were to reverse the expansion of mind and heart that education is meant to accomplish—to turn poetry into jargon, music into discord, and wine into water. For everything appears small and flat and gray in the dim light of cultural repudiation. Heroic greatness of soul is reduced to toxic masculinity. Beauty is understood to be a construction of whiteness, and mathematics, the glory of pure intellect, an instrument of cultural subjugation. Intellectual humility and interpretive charity, tried-and-true gateways to surpassing wonders, are in many universities as dispensable as ancient languages are for classics majors at Princeton, or Chaucer and Shakespeare for English majors at Yale.

This is not all. In Plato's Cave image, the would-be educator receives no hearing. He confronts a chorus of hostility and derision and is accused of corrupting souls. Similarly, speakers, professors, and students who challenge political and intellectual orthodoxy in our universities—generally advancing views, incidentally, that most Americans find uncontroversial—are regularly disinvited, slandered, and sometimes fired simply because of the opinions they hold, the questions they ask, or the arguments they make. Little wonder that more than 80 percent of college students report self-censoring.

In brief, a crisis of illiberalism engulfs American higher education. Wherever the free exchange of ideas is discouraged, wherever intellectual pluralism is suppressed, the pursuit of truth is crippled and thought deformed. But it's not just students who are shortchanged. Life in general becomes more solitary, impoverished, and brutish. These are symptoms of incipient societal osteoporosis, which, in the worst case, culminates in fractures of the civilizational backbone.

This is what happened during the French Revolution, when the National Assembly reset the calendar to the Year One, and in Cambodia, where the Khmer Rouge, not to be outdone in cultural repudiation, began at Year Zero. At such times, thought and imagination shrivel, like a plant cut off at the root. Neighbor turns against neighbor, and individuals, overcome by anxiety and depression, turn against themselves. And while ideological tyranny and societal collapse may seem like remote possibilities in the United States, too much of our common life looks like what historian Niall Ferguson calls Totalitarianism Lite.

To be clear, the picture I've just sketched reflects my own views. My colleagues at UATX, commonly known as the University of Austin, would doubtless describe things differently, though I wouldn't be surprised if most agreed with much of what I've said. In any case, we are united in our belief that higher education needs radical reform and that the best way forward is to start a new university.

Let me say something about who we are, what new ideas we plan to implement, and why I think we can have a major impact on higher education.

Our guiding principles are few but firm. We have faith in the process of liberal education—in the capacity of individuals to discover truth and attain freedom through the unfettered examination and open discussion of fundamental human questions. We are committed to high standards of academic rigor. We believe that students can learn, and professors can teach, only if they are free to ask questions and share opinions without fear. We are committed to freedom of inquiry, freedom of conscience, and civil discourse, without which truth is eclipsed and education decays into indoctrination.

Free and open debate, however, is not a sufficient condition of teaching and learning. We are guided by a robust conception of human flourishing. We believe that a rigorous education reveals the basic stuff of our being and equips us to pursue what we love and do well. We seek to cultivate excellence as the condition of meaningful freedom: the power to do good, honor truth, and nurture beauty.

We want our students to understand the foundations and blessings of civilization and political life, to grasp the importance of law, virtue, order, beauty, meaningful work and leisure, and the sacred. We want them to appreciate the unique vibrancy of the American form of government and way of life. We want them to become conversant in the various languages of understanding and to learn to advance ideas and arguments logically and lucidly in speech and writing. We especially want them to develop prudence, which requires seeing things whole, making connections, and sorting signal from noise across multiple domains of experience.

We believe that politics should be a subject of study in a university, not its operating system.

We reject partisan politics and the ideological invasion of the classroom and the laboratory. As an institution, we will not publicly endorse or promote political positions.

Students need a dedicated space in which to grow and ripen. They need to be disentangled from the urgencies of the here and now. We therefore embrace the idea of the university as a tower—not of ivory but of glass. From within the tower, it must be possible to observe and reflect on society; and from without, to see what goes on inside it. Radical transparency, not a value of most universities, is essential to everything we do.

UATX aspires to revitalize American higher education as a steward of tradition and an engine of innovation. This combination, which recalls the Roman god Janus, who looks backward and forward simultaneously, makes for a creative tension. Tradition without innovation tends toward sterility; soil is fertile only to the extent that it is enriched by the decayed residue of new growths. Innovation without tradition is blind; it tends to repeat the mistakes of the past while falling short of its successes.

A UATX degree will not, at first, have the cachet of an Ivy League school. But "we don't sell credential, we develop potential," as our founding president, Pano Kanelos, recently remarked. And we propose to offer a genuinely liberal and liberating education at half the cost of elite colleges and universities. How?

First, we will have a low administrative footprint and guard against administrative bloat. We will outsource as many tasks as possible to private entities and individuals. Higher-level on-campus administrative positions, like head librarian or registrar, will, as far as possible, be filled by Ph.D.s competent to teach in our academic programs. We will forgo the usual Club-Med student amenities. We won't have expensive intercollegiate athletics. We are researching ways to introduce economic efficiencies into administration, such as giving academic units direct control over and responsibility for their budgets.

"In a university, all contested questions deserve a hearing. If students read Hayek, they should read Marx."

We will channel the money we save on administration and nonacademic amenities toward instruction. These cost-saving measures will strengthen our academic programs and help us attract good students. Financially unstable universities inevitably erode academically. They chase income wherever they can find it, regardless of academic quality, and replace seasoned professors with poorly paid and overworked adjuncts.

We care about academic freedom and have taken steps to preserve it. To begin with, we will not offer tenure. Tenure is supposed to protect academic freedom, but today it has paradoxically led to narrowing the confines of acceptable opinion and has encouraged political conformity. In the humanities and social sciences, as several surveys have shown, self-identified liberals outnumber conservatives 12 to one and are far less open to opposing political viewpoints than the general public. What is more, universities increasingly require Diversity, Equity, and Inclusion oaths for tenure-track jobs and tenure in all academic fields, including those in STEM. For these reasons, conservatives are unlikely to be hired and even less likely to receive tenure.

We find this undesirable not because we are an institution of the Right. We are not. We are trans-political. It is because, in a university, all sides of every contested question deserve a hearing. If students read Friedrich Hayek, they should read Karl Marx—and vice versa. We propose to advance intellectual pluralism and avoid ideological sclerosis by offering graduated-term contracts with specifiable deliverables. To reward those willing to risk working without the protection of tenure, we will have low course loads and pay extremely competitive salaries. And if issues of academic freedom do arise, we plan to submit them to an Academic Freedom Review Board external to the university, with whose judgment we are pledged to abide.

What about our curriculum?

We begin with Intellectual Foundations (IF), a core liberal arts program required of all undergraduates in their first two years. IF seminars, complemented by common lectures that draw connections across different courses, will emphasize writing and discussion. Courses include "Chaos and Civilization"; "Knowing, Doing, Making, Wisdom"; "Writing and the English Language"; "Quantitative Reasoning I and II"; "The Beginning of Politics"; "Christianity and Islam, Europe and the East"; "Intellectual Foundations of Economics"; "Modernity and the West"; "Work, Leisure, and the Good Life"; "The Uses and Abuses of Technology"; "The American Experiment I and II"; "The Sublime and the Beautiful"; "Ideological Experiments of the Twentieth Century"; and "Mortality and Meaning, God and Suffering." Readings range from Homer, Euclid, Genesis, the Gospel of John, Ibn Tufayl, and Confucius to Descartes, Tocqueville, Orwell, Frederick Douglass, and Flannery O'Connor.

By the time students enter their junior year, they will have several intellectual Velcro hooks with which they can grab on to any new subject. That will be crucial as they enter one of our Centers of Inquiry—Arts and Letters; Politics, Economics and History; Science, Technology, Engineering and Mathematics; Education and Public Service—and begin to concentrate on another distinctive element of our curriculum, the Polaris Projects. These projects involve doing, making, building, or discovering something of general benefit. Like the North Star, they are meant to orient a student's education and give it an overall trajectory. Polaris Projects can be creative, scholarly, technical, artistic, philanthropic, entrepreneurial—the list is not exhaustive. But all will involve connecting with people and employing resources outside the university.

Our students may not always bring these projects to fruition. But the process of seeing a human need, drafting plans, formulating and reformulating goals and means, researching and experimenting, and trying and failing will prepare them to be thoughtful innovators and builders. It will teach them how to work cooperatively; how to research precedents and identify best practices; how to form and leverage connections; and how to plan, execute, assess, and publicly present their own work. It will prepare them for life.

I believe that UATX will help rescue American higher education for two reasons.

First, we will succeed. The demand for authentic education far exceeds the supply. We proved that with our Forbidden Courses program this past

June, which attracted exceptionally capable and broad-minded students to study subjects like religion, feminism, capitalism, and ideology with cultural and intellectual leaders like Ayaan Hirsi Ali, Niall Ferguson, and Deirdre McCloskey. Our students wrote widely circulated and laudatory articles about their experience. Forbidden Courses alumni spontaneously formed a Student Advisory Board for UATX and held elections for officers.

Our outstanding team of trustees and advisors includes leaders in politics, business, culture, the arts, and the academy. We have received more than 5,000 job inquiries from professors and thousands of inquiries from students. And fund-raising is going extremely well. In the first ten months after the public announcement of UATX, we gained more than 1,500 individual donors, more than 60 of whom made gifts of six, seven, or eight figures, and we're on track to hit our capital campaign target a year early. This is really happening.

Second, success breeds imitation. UATX will still be in the process of acquiring accreditation when our initial class of undergraduate students graduates (this is, in fact, how the process works). These first students will be risk-takers who want an education more than a credential. These are the kinds of people who become innovators and builders. They will make their mark in many fields, including the rapidly changing arena of education—and when they do, the world will take notice.

Infectious excitement is a natural consequence of intellectual invigoration. "You've given us a sense of hope," one Forbidden Courses alum wrote, "and that hope and incredible vision has spread all the way to Dublin, Ireland, where I applied from." Another called UATX "one of the most exciting developments in American education and intellectual life," while a third wrote that "UATX has renewed my faith in the future of academia." I have no doubt that our example will encourage a new generation of educational entrepreneurs to found colleges and universities worthy of such hope and faith: places where teaching and learning will again flourish.

Appendix

Abolish DEI Bureaucracies and Restore Colorblind Equality in Public Universities – Manhattan Institute: https://manhattan.institute/article/abolish-dei-bureaucracies-and-restore-colorblind-equality-in-public-universities

Alumni Free Speech Alliance (AFSA) members:

- Bucknell: Open Discourse Coalition
- Cornell: Cornell Free Speech Alliance
- Davidson: Davidsonians for Freedom of Thought & Discourse
- Harvard: Harvard Alumni for Free Speech
- Lafayette: Alumni/Alumnae Coalition for Lafayette
- Massachusetts Institute of Technology: MIT Free Speech Alliance
- Princeton: Princetonians for Free Speech
- University of North Carolina: UNC Free Speech Alliance
- University of Virginia: The Jefferson Council
- Virginia Military Institute: The Spirit of VMI
- Washington & Lee: The Generals Redoubt
- Wofford: Alumni for the Wofford Way
- Yale: Fight for Yale's Future

DEI Has Corrupted the Public Universities—And Must Be Abolished – Video by Christopher F. Rufo from the Manhattan Institute: https://www.youtube.com/watch?v=nw4BBQb71bg.

Free Speech Alumni Ambassador (FSAA) Program Handbook – S.A.P.I.E.N.T. Being: https://www.sapientbeing.org/_files/ugd/3c625c_f21c8a06057d43a7974cfd409ab6a036.pdf.

References

Alumni Free Speech Alliance (AFSA): https://alumnifreespeechalliance.com/

Alumni Withhold Donations, Demand Colleges Enforce Free Speech *Wall Street Journal* 11-30-21 https://dftdunite.org/alumni-withhold-donations-demand-colleges-enforce-free-speech.

American Council of Trustees and Alumni (ACTA): https://www.goacta.org/issues/academic-freedom/.

Buck, Daniel and Garion Frankel. "How Public Schools Went Woke—and What to Do About It." *National Review*. March 5, 2022. https://www.nationalreview.com/2022/03/how-public-schools-went-woke-and-what-to-do-about-it/.

Chicago Statement on Freedom of Expression: https://www.thefire.org/research-learn/adopting-chicago-statement.

Downey, Caroline. *National Review*. Harvard Alums Run Outsider Campaign to Overhaul Presidential Selection Process, Eliminate DEI. January 31, 2024. https://www.nationalreview.com/news/harvard-alums-run-outsider-campaign-to-overhaul-presidential-selection-process-eliminate-dei/.

Free Speech Alumni Ambassador (FSAA) Program Handbook. S.A.P.I.E.N.T. Being. June 23, 2023. https://www.sapientbeing.org/_files/ugd/3c625c_f21c8a06057d43a7974cfd409ab6a036.pdf.

Gold, Howard. "Opinion: At America's most 'woke' colleges, extreme liberal politics fails students and free speech." Market Watch. January 27, 2020. https://www.marketwatch.com/story/at-americas-most-woke-colleges-extreme-liberal-politics-fails-students-and-free-speech-2020-01-27.

Gonzalez, Mike. "Seizing the Moment." *City Journal*. Oct. 27, 2023. https://www.city-journal.org/article/how-conservatives-can-push-back-against-woke.

Gulliver, Katrina. "Cancelling the Cancellers." *City Journal*. Oct. 13, 2023. https://www.city-journal.org/article/cancelling-the-cancellers.

Haidt, Dr. Jonathan. "Viewpoint Diversity in the Academy." www.righteousmind.com. 2019.

Haidt, Jonathan and Greg Lukianoff. *The Coddling of the American Mind: How Good Intentions and Bad Ideas Are Setting Up a Generation for Failure*. Penguin Random House: New York. 2018.

Haidt, Jonathan. "Why Universities Must Choose One Telos: Truth or Social Justice." Heterodox Academy. October 21, 2017. https://heterodoxacademy.org/blog/one-telos-truth-or-social-justice-2/.

How Alumni Can Organize to Support Free Speech and Academic Freedom At Their College or University. Alumni Free Speech Alliance. June 3, 2022. https://alumnifreespeechalliance.com/.

Howland, Jacob. "College of the Future." *City Journal*. Winter 2023. https://www.city-journal.org/article/college-of-the-future.

Howland, Jacob. "The Campus Peril to Western Civilization." *City Journal*. Oct. 22 2023. https://www.city-journal.org/article/the-campus-peril-to-western-civilization.

Kalven Report. University of Chicago. 1967. https://provost.uchicago.edu/sites/default/files/documents/reports/KalvenRprt_0.pdf.

Kupfer, Theodore. "Where Did Wokeness Come From?" *City Journal*. Aug. 19, 2022. https://www.city-journal.org/article/where-did-wokeness-come-from.

Leibovitz, Liel. "The Big University Fail." City Journal. Dec. 6, 2023. https://www.city-journal.org/article/the-big-university-fail.

Leroux, Robert. "Woke Madness and the University." National Association of Scholars. Winter 2021. https://www.NAS.org/academic-questions/34/4/woke-madness-and-the-university.

Lukianoff, Greg and Rikki Schlott. *The Canceling of the American Mind: Cancel Culture Undermines Trust and Threatens Us All—But There Is a Solution*. Simon & Schuster, New York. 2023.

Mac Donald, Heather. "The Academy at the Crossroads, Part Two: Penn 2.0 and the larger ideological problem: universities are waging a war on the West." *City Journal*. Dec. 14 2023. https://www.city-journal.org/article/the-academy-at-the-crossroads-part-two.

Manning, Teresa R. "A New Bill Offers Hope of Protecting Free-Speech Rights at American Universities." City Journal. September 22, 2021. https://www.city-journal.org/can-legislation-protect-free-speech-on-campus.

Miller, Wade and Dan Morenoff, Ilya Shapiro, David E. Bernstein, James Sherk, Judge Glock, Christopher F. Rufo. "How to Defeat Left-Wing Racialism." *City*

156

Journal. Summer 2023. https://www.city-journal.org/article/how-to-defeat-left-wing-racialism.

Murnane, Connor. "Alumni Take Up the Fight for Free Speech—and You Can Help!" FIRE. October 21, 2021. https://www.thefire.org/alumni-take-up-the-fight-for-free-speech-and-you-can-help/.

National Suicide by Education—Care of Progressives. *The S.A.P.I.E.N.T. Being Newsletter.* Sep. 20, 2023. https://www.sapientbeing.org/so/39OPtaY7w?languageTag=en.

Patai, Daphne. "How a University Moved From Diversity to Indoctrination." Minding the Campus. December 11, 2016. https://shoutout.wix.com/so/89OEfLxMs?languageTag=en#/main.

Rufo, Christopher F. "Banging Beyond Binaries." *City Journal.* May 17, 2022. https://www.city-journal.org/philadelphia-schools-tout-radical-transgender-conference.

Rufo, Christopher F. "Giving DEI the Pink Slip." *City Journal.* Mar. 4, 2024 https://www.city-journal.org/article/giving-dei-the-pink-slip.

Rufo, Christopher F. "Radical Gender Lessons for Young Children." *City Journal.* April 21, 2022. https://www.city-journal.org/radical-gender-lessons-for-young-children.

Rufo, Christopher F. "Sexual Liberation in Public Schools." *City Journal.* July 20, 2022. https://www.city-journal.org/sexual-liberation-in-public-schools.

Sailer, John D. and Ray M. Sanchez. "An Overt Political Litmus Test." *City Journal.* May 16, 2022. https://www.city-journal.org/california-community-colleges-impose-political-litmus-test.

Salzman, Philip Carl. "What Happened to Our Universities?" Minding the Campus. October 2018. https://www.mindingthecampus.org/2018/10/31/what-happened-to-our-universities/.

Sanzi, Erika. "The Monster Is in the Classroom." *City Journal.* April 30, 2021. https://www.city-journal.org/elementary-schools-go-woke.

Schalin, Jay. "Bolstering the Board: Trustees Are Academia's Best Hope for Reform." James G. Martin Center for Academic Renewal. July 14, 2020. https://www.jamesgmartin.center/2020/07/bolstering-the-board-trustees-are-academias-best-hope-for-reform/.

Schalin, Jay. "Bolstering the Board: Trustees Are Academia's Best Hope for Reform." The James G. Martin Center for Academic Renewal. July 14, 2020.

https://www.jamesgmartin.center/2020/07/bolstering-the-board-trustees-are-academias-best-hope-for-reform/.

Spotlight on Speech Codes F.I.R.E. 2022. Foundation for Individual Rights and Expression (F.I.R.E.). https://www.thefire.org/resources/spotlight/reports/spotlight-on-speech-codes-2022/.

Statement of Principles on Academic Freedom and Tenure. American Association of University Professors. 1940. https://www.aaup.org/report/1940-statement-principles-academic-freedom-and-tenure.

Thomas, Bradley. "Statistical Disparities Among Groups Are Not Proof of Discrimination." Foundation for Economic Education (FEE). May 21, 2019. https://fee.org/articles/statistical-disparities-among-groups-are-not-proof-of-discrimination/?itm_source=parsely-api.

Wilson, Corey Lee. *Progressivism Madness: A SAPIENT Being's Guide to the Idiocracy and Hypocrisy of the 'Regressivism' Movement*. Corona, CA: Fratire Publishing. 2023.

Wilson, Corey Lee. *The S.A.P.I.E.N.T. Being: A Critical Thinking Guide to Help Stop & Prevent Academia's Neo-Marxist & Racist Progressivist Agenda*. Corona, CA: Fratire Publishing. 2023, 2nd edition.

Wood, Alan. "DEI Exposed: The Dangers of Forced Conformity in Diversity Equity & Inclusion." Global Watchdog. March 13, 2024. https://gwmac.com/dei-exposed-forced-conformity/.

Woodward Report. Yale University. 1974. https://yalecollege.yale.edu/get-know-yale-college/office-dean/reports/report-committee-freedom-expression-yale.

Yenor, Scott. "How Red-State Universities Evade DEI Restrictions." *City Journal*. Sep. 26, 2023. https://www.city-journal.org/article/how-red-state-universities-evade-dei-restrictions.

Index

Author Bio

Corey Lee Wilson

Corey Lee Wilson was raised an atheist by his liberal *Playboy* Bunny mother, has three Anglo-Hispanic siblings, a bi-racial daughter, a brother who died of AIDS, baptized a Protestant by his conservative grandparents, attended temple with his Jewish foster parents, baptized again as a Catholic for his first Filipina wife, attends Buddhist ceremonies with his second Thai wife, became an agnostic on his own free will for most of his life, and is a lifetime independent voter.

Corey felt the sting of intellectual humility by repeating the 4th grade and attended eighteen different schools (17 in California and one in the Bahamas) before putting himself through college (without parents) at Mt. San Antonio College and Cal Poly Pomona University (while on triple secret probation).

Named Who's Who of American College Students in 1984, he received a BS in Economics (summa cum laude) and won his fraternity's most prestigious undergraduate honor, the Phi Kappa Tau Fraternity's Shideler Award, both in 1985. In 2020, he became a member of the Heterodox Academy, in 2021 a member of the National Association of Scholars and 1776 Unites, and in 2023 became a member of Moms for Liberty.

As a satirist and fraternity man, Corey started Fratire Publishing in 2012 and transformed the fiction "fratire" genre to a respectable and viewpoint diverse nonfiction genre promoting practical knowledge and wisdom to help everyday people navigate safely through the many hazards of life. In 2019, he founded the S.A.P.I.E.N.T. Being to help promote freedom of speech, viewpoint diversity, intellectual humility and most importantly advance sapience in America's students and campuses.

Some readers might be prone to ask why would someone raised as a wild-hippy-gypsy child of the Sixties take the conservative path and champion conservative causes?

Quick answer: In this day and age it's the reasonable, logical, and sapient thing to do. By comparison, there is nothing "sapient" about the Progressivism movement and the woke madness that follows it throughout our educational systems.

Furthermore, to quote Ronald Reagan, "There's a flickering spark in us all which, if struck at just the right age, can light the rest of our lives." His spark was ignited in college when he experienced first-hand in the early Eighties the growing illiberalism at his college newspaper and its persistent bias against conservatives, Christians, and President Reagan.

Hopefully, this *Woke Free Campus Guide* will do the same to spark your inspiration to help undue the societal destruction of DEI and the leftist woke madness that follows on your campus. Better yet, use this sapient guidebook to champion and craft your own anti-wokeness platform and winning strategy for campus student government elections.